MW01075767

I AIN'T GOT TIRED YET
The Spiritual Battles of Enslaved African Christians and their Descendants

By: Mark P. Fancher

Copyright 2010 Mark P. Fancher

Africanalysis Books
P.O. Box 4112
Ann Arbor, MI 48106

I been in de war so long, I ain't got tired yit
I been in de war so long, I ain't got tired yit
Well, my head been wet wid de midnight dew
The 'fo' day star was a witness too
I been in de war so long en I ain't got tired yit
My knees is acquainted wid de hillside clay
Ain't got tired yit
Feet placed on de rock of eternitay
Ain't got tired yit

Ole Satan is mad en I am glad
Ain't got tired yit
Missed a soul he thought he had
En I ain't got tired yit

Oh, been in de war so long, ain't got tired yit
Oh, been in de war so long, ain't got tired yit

Table of Contents

Appendix of Essays on African Dignity, Character and Self-Respect

3

Praise God, Our Father

Author's Note

This book is a spiritual analysis, but I am neither a trained theologian, nor a divinely inspired prophet. My credentials for writing this book rest entirely on my belief that because God intended everyone - even those who never attended a seminary- to be guided by the Bible as the divinely inspired word of God, then it needs no interpretation by scholars.

I begin and end with a presumption that scriptures must be taken literally no matter how much skepticism or discomfort they may cause. God makes no mistakes, and therefore, every line of scripture has been written in precisely the manner he intended. Many have helped me to gain insight into the word of God, but if I have made any errors in Biblical analysis in this volume, I believe those mistakes are due to my own failure (or unwillingness) to accept the scriptures precisely as they are written.

Chapter One

God's Special Relationship With The Oppressed

While enveloped by inky blackness, writhing Africans pulled and twisted wrists and ankles in desperate attempts to slip from the shackles that bound them in the holds of slave ships sailing to destinations unknown. Metal bands cut deeply into raw, sweaty flesh, but the captives welcomed the flow of blood and hoped that it might serve as a liberating lubricant. These Africans taken from their home continent, along with their countless descendants, were destined to live lives of struggle.

Slave ship uprisings, plantation rebellions, runaway slaves, maroon wars, abolitionist organizing, back-to-Africa campaigns, civil disobedience, freedom rides, urban insurrections, guerrilla warfare, electoral campaigns, human rights conferences, and many other acts of resistance are at the very heart of the African sojourn in the western hemisphere. While these flesh and blood efforts to win freedom are the backdrop for this book, spiritual battles are the primary focus.

Spiritual conflict is not always tangible because it involves the ongoing war between God and the good that he represents and Satan and the evil that he creates. Each side seeks to dominate the universe, and on earth strategic priority is given by both opposing forces to entering into the hearts, souls and minds of human beings.

Material struggles, where blows are exchanged, or bullets are fired, or miles are marched, or where votes are cast are not always disconnected from spiritual warfare. In the spiritual realm, where God and his angels fight the Satanic forces of hell, conflicts spill over into daily earthly affairs, and often manifest themselves in the form of battles by warring parties to either promote or eradicate racial oppression and discrimination. Africans of the diaspora are a longstanding focal point of these conflicts on earth, and these beleaguered, resilient and noble people have effectively fought back, not only by putting their bodies in harm's way, but also with prayer, prophetic witnessing and a rock solid unshakeable faith. It is the spiritual element of Africans' resistance that has arguably preserved them as a people under conditions that might have wiped out others with less faith. More remarkable still has been the ability of Africans in the diaspora to not only survive, but in many cases to prevail.

Spiritual warfare may occur instinctively and without deliberation, but Africa's diaspora has produced countless conscious warriors who, like Bob Marley "... did not come to fight flesh and blood, but spiritual wickedness in high and low places." Students of liberation struggles that have been waged in the African diaspora err when they neglect to study and analyze the spiritual dimension. This is true because so many Africans who have played pivotal roles in these struggles understood that their success depended less upon their ability to physically overcome their oppressors than it did upon defeating evil as a force that animated those who were responsible for the oppression that they fought to eliminate.

This book's analysis of the African diaspora's spiritual warriors and their battles demands that readers do two things. First, all questions, concerns and disbelief about the absolute accuracy of the entire Biblical text must be suspended, and all scriptures must be accepted as true. Second, the Bible must at all times be considered as a single, indivisible document. In other words, one cannot choose to analyze one section of the Bible and then ignore the balance of the text. For purposes of this book, the entire Bible must be read as one would read a novel. A reader would not read the middle 70 pages of *Native Son*, and feel secure that he or she knows the full story.

Though readers are asked to presume for the sake of discussion and analysis that, among other things, God created the earth in seven days, they are not asked to, in their secular lives, ignore evolution or the numerous scientific and historical studies that some contend contradict various Biblical passages. The point is that when attempting to discern the spiritual truth that the Bible communicates, scientific and historical studies can create obstacles to profound understanding.

When communicating spiritual truth, it is not at all important that events described in a lesson be actual historical occurrences. For example, in order to convey moral teachings, Jesus himself frequently used parables. The lessons of these parables would have been missed if listeners had been unwilling to hear the stories as Jesus told them. If, for example, Jesus' audience had become preoccupied with whether the good Samaritan was an actual person or a fictional character, they might easily have missed the whole point of the story. Likewise, for the Bible to communicate a spiritual truth that makes sense, the facts in the narrative must be accepted as presented. Whether Shadrach, Meshach and Abednego were actually cast into a fiery furnace is unimportant to understanding the spiritual lesson that their story teaches.

The Bible speaks repeatedly of the special spiritual status of those who have been damned, despised, oppressed and condemned to lives of poverty. Africa's diaspora is certainly in that category. These Africans' story is filled with misery.

Africans locked in the holds of slave ships like sardines literally swimming in bodily waste and excretions for weeks and months; unspeakable plantation tortures; lynching; bombings; rapes; dismemberment; harassment; discrimination; and more have left a legacy of blood and tears from which many Africans have not begun to recover.

When confronted by facts about such suffering, believers and non-believers alike ask why a loving and all-powerful God allows such in a world that he created. How can God stand by and do nothing to protect innocents? Why does God allow the wicked to prosper with impunity? These questions are likely to continue to perplex even the most devout believers until they truly understand that not only is God not the cause of the earth's suffering, but that he is actually engaged in an ongoing high intensity, no-holds-barred war against spiritual forces of evil that are in fact responsible for human misery.

If anyone has any doubts at all about what God intends for humanity, they need only consider that in Genesis, God established for human beings a perfect paradise. That stands as the most powerful evidence of what God actually wants for us. He wants us to live in a perfect world. Many forget that it was Satan - not God - who poisoned Eden with evil, effectively firing the first shot in a battle for control of earth that was to extend through the millennia.

Since the fall of Adam and Eve, God has been engaged in a fierce struggle to purge the planet of Satan's taint. On earth, this struggle has taken many forms depending largely upon the extent and nature of the evil threat. Satan's grip on the planet during the earliest portions of the Old Testament was quite strong. Entire populations and societies were essentially possessed by evil, and God's only alternative was to empower a chosen community to fight a long series of some of the bloodiest physical battles ever recorded.

The accounts of these battles are very troubling to many because they suggest a violent, angry, bloodthirsty deity who is very different from the popular image of God as a gentle, kindly, benevolent father figure. If, as is urged by this book, the reader takes the scriptures at face value and in their totality, God appears to be neither bloodthirsty nor passive. He does appear to be a God who loves humanity passionately and who is not in the least reluctant to - like Malcolm X - protect the human family "by any means necessary." Thus, the Old Testament chronicles not only violent military campaigns carried out by God's soldiers, but also a flood and other natural disasters that were designed to purge the planet of irredeemable populations that would otherwise forever stand in the way of the re-establishment

11

of paradise.

The tumultuous conflicts of the Old Testament were in large measure successful. As decency regained its traction on earth, the number of epic, cataclysmic physical battles began to diminish and the war moved into the spiritual realm. Prophets emerged who began to articulate moral and ethical observations that struck at the very heart of satanic doctrines. Though in many cases these prophets suffered physical retaliation, it became increasingly clear that their physical presence was less threatening than their spiritual power, and for the forces of evil, simple assassination was an ineffective response.

The prophets brought greater clarity to humanity about what God needed and expected from his children. Ultimately, however, it took the "Son of God" to break Satan's lock on earthly affairs by explaining in the most clear and direct way the precise role of humanity in the universal struggle against evil. Though God had at his disposal legions of angels who could have engaged Satan directly, he instead gave Jesus the role of gladiator whose mission was to fight a winner-take-all battle against the evil foe. This battle was fought, not by way of physical combat, but instead through a test of wills.

In the opening skirmishes, Satan attempted to tempt Jesus in the desert. This was a return to the tactic used successfully against Adam and Eve when evil was first introduced into the earthly realm. When temptation failed, Satan employed every other weapon in his arsenal, and by working through human surrogates confronted Jesus with jealousy, betrayal, greed, vengeance, and extreme torture. Finally, when left with nothing else that could stop God's power, Satan killed the human vessel. As every Christian knows, even this failed, and Jesus' resurrection served as a signal that the message delivered by the Messiah was the one that can liberate every believer from Satan's grip if only they choose to hear, have faith and act according to Christ's teachings.

As liberating as it was, the resurrection could not be the trigger for the restoration of the Garden of Eden. This is because the foibles, failings and errors of the masses in the period leading up to the crucifixion brought into even sharper focus the fact that the souls of humanity had become not only flawed, but disgustingly soiled by Satan's influence. Unlike the newly-created virtuous and pure Adam and Eve, the human species was no longer suited for the role of caretaker of God's paradise. Thus, Jesus could only establish a framework for individual redemption. Whether individuals were suited for paradise was now to be determined on a case-by-case basis. What this means in practical terms is that since the resurrection, the question for each human has been whether he or she is up to the challenge spelled out by Jesus during his ministry. It is not as easy a challenge as most Christians would like to believe. In his book *The Politics of Jesus*, author Obery Hendricks observes:

> For all of his moral and ethical teachings in the Beatitudes and the parables and in his instructions to his disciples and others, Jesus gave just one criterion for judging the righteousness of our lives: 'Then he will say to those at his left hand, 'You that are accursed, depart from me...for I was hungry and you gave me no food. I was thirsty and you gave me nothing to drink, I was a stranger and you did not welcome me, naked and you did not give me clothing, sick and in prison and you did not visit me.' Then they...will answer, 'Lord, when was it that we saw you hungry or thirsty or a stranger or naked or sick or in prison, and did not take care of you?' Then he will answer them, 'Truly I tell you, just as you did not do it to one of the least of these, you did not do it to me.' And these will go away into eternal punishment, but the righteous into eternal life.' (Matthew 25:41-46) By the measure Jesus gives us here, it is not religious practice, or memorization of scriptures, or even faithful attendance at church or temple by which our lives are judged. It is simply this: whether we have tried to relieve the plight of the hungry and dispossessed and those stripped of their freedom; whether we have tried to change this war-torn world to a world free from oppression and exploitation, so that all of God's children might

14

have life, and that more abundantly.[1]

Recognizing that those who fight for justice in the way that Hendricks suggests are almost certain to encounter resistance and retaliation, Jesus calmed their fears. He stated: "Blessed are ye when men shall hate you, and when they shall separate you from their company, and shall reproach you, and cast out your name as evil, for the Son of Man's sake. Rejoice ye in that day, and leap for joy; for behold, your reward is great in heaven; for in the like manner did their fathers unto the prophets." Luke 6:22-23.

Jesus also made it abundantly clear that the poor and oppressed were not merely the objects of the benevolence of the righteous. Of all humanity, they possessed the golden ticket to Heaven. "Blessed be ye poor; for yours is the kingdom of God. Blessed are ye that hunger now; for ye shall be filled. Blessed are ye that weep now; for ye shall laugh." Luke 6:20-21.

Why would God insist on limiting salvation only to those who have suffered and to those who have struggled to eliminate the suffering of others? It has everything to do with the strength, caliber and quality of the souls that God not only wants, but needs as he and his angels engage in ongoing spiritual warfare against the forces of darkness. In the struggle with Satan over who will have dominion over the earth, God often fights through surrogates that are either human, or that have human form. We have already considered the deadly dance of sorts between Jesus and Satan, where success in a high stakes conflict depended entirely on the incorruptibility of Jesus the gladiator. This encounter was not unique. In the Book of Job, we get a pretty clear picture of how the ongoing contest between Satan and God's soldiers plays itself out.

In the opening chapter of Job, God is essentially reviewing his troops of angels when, uninvited and unwanted, Satan appears in their midst. God asks from whence he has come, and Satan explains that he has been wandering the earth, presumably in search of opportunities to make mischief. We can assume that it would have been possible for God to attack Satan directly – as the intruder stood in enemy territory. However, it is necessary for God to allow those who inhabit the earth in physical form to carry the flag for the Lord. This is because while ultimately, even if humanity purifies itself, new-found purity will be for nought if people are shielded by God from Satan's influence and they never have the opportunity to develop their own armor of virtue and moral toughness.

Satan knows that his control of the earth is assured as long as he has access to humans who are vulnerable to corruption. So in order for God to win and maintain dominion over the planet, God's people must demonstrate definitively that they cannot be lured into subversion. Thus, rather than engage Satan directly, God challenges Satan to take his best shots at Job, one of his most faithful servants. As we know, Satan was defeated badly in that contest by a morally tough human being.

There are only certain types of human beings who develop Job's toughness, and they are the people who are repeatedly identified in the Bible as those who have the greatest favor with God. These are victims of terrible tragedies, the poor, the damned, the despised, and those who struggle on behalf of these outcasts and suffer terrible consequences for their efforts. God calls these individuals into his presence, even in the Heavenly realm because his struggle against evil is not limited to the planet earth. It is universal in scope.

For a clearer picture of the relationship between God and the poor and tormented souls that are welcomed into his Heavenly presence, reference can be made to Revelation 7. John, the author, reports:

> After this I beheld, and, lo, a great multitude which no man could number, of all nations, and kindreds, and people and tongues, stood before the throne, and before the Lamb, clothed with white robes, and palms in their hands. And cried

17

with a loud voice, saying, Salvation to our God which sitteth upon the throne, and unto the Lamb. And all the angels stood round about the throne, and about the elders and the four beasts, and fell before the throne on their faces and worshiped God. Saying, Amen: Blessing and glory, and wisdom, and thanksgiving, and honor, and power and might be unto our God for ever and ever. Amen. And one of the elders answered, saying unto me, What are these which are arrayed in white robes? and whence came they? And I said unto him, Sir, thou knowest. And he said to me, These are they which came out of great tribulation, and have washed their robes, and made them white in the blood of the Lamb. Therefore are they before the throne of God and serve him day and night in his temple: and he that sitteth on the throne shall dwell among them. They shall hunger no more, neither thirst any more; neither shall the sun light on them, nor any heat. For the Lamb which is in the midst of the throne shall feed them, and shall lead them unto living fountains of waters: and God shall wipe away all tears from their eyes.

A God who has been fighting a war, has little interest in rewarding the spiritually indolent, or surrounding himself with pampered, lazy, untested souls who never resisted the Satanic foe. The saints who are closest to the throne are those who endured "great tribulation." These are individuals who were tested in the fire and whose souls emerged intact absolutely committed to the Lord. They do not spend their time lounging. Instead they "serve [God] day and night" likely by generating heavy duty spiritual energy that maintains God's dominance over evil. It is energy of a type that perhaps no one but an individual who has endured "great tribulation" would have. Many in the ranks of oppressed humanity have endured their share of tribulation, even before the unfolding of the cataclysmic events described in Revelation, and they would fit in very well with those who reside next to God's throne because of their unswerving commitment to their Lord even as they suffered. This is perhaps why Jesus insisted so vehemently that the poor and oppressed and others who experience such hardship and who are so pitied on earth are actually the most blessed.

From Genesis to Revelation, the Bible chronicles the raging war, but because there are not constant explicit references to actual confrontations between God and Satan, it is not readily apparent to the casual reader that this conflict is central to the accounts of the foibles, heroism and moral dilemmas that are played out by Biblical personalities. Further confusion results from the fact that the battles in this spiritual war frequently bear little resemblance to the earthly wars that define such conflicts for most people. The most important and most intense battles fought by Jesus did not involve physical violence, even though the circumstances surrounding these conflicts would have prompted many humans to resort to physical retaliation.

Contrary to widely-held beliefs, the scriptures suggest that Jesus was not a pacifist. There is of course the episode popularly known as the "cleansing of the temple" when Jesus goes on a rampage, physically destroying merchants' sales stations and ejecting them from the premises with a whip of cords. Then, when anticipating a showdown with the authorities, Jesus instructs his disciples to arm themselves. Luke 22:36 - 38 states: "Then said he unto them, But now, he that hath a purse, let him take it, and likewise, his scrip; and he that hath no sword, let him sell his garment, and buy one. For I say unto you, that this that is written must yet be accomplished in me. And he was reckoned among the transgressors; for the things concerning me have an end. And they said, Lord behold, here are two swords. And he said unto them, It is enough."

Nevertheless, when the effort was made to arrest Jesus in the Garden of Gethsemane, and a disciple dutifully drew his blade and sliced off a soldier's ear, Jesus implored him to put the weapon away, saying: "Put up again thy sword into his place; for all they that take the sword shall perish with the sword. Thinkest thou that I cannot now pray to my Father, and he shall presently give me more than twelve legions of angels? But how then shall

20

the scriptures be fulfilled, that thus it must be?" Matthew 26:52-54.

This incident is highly instructive for several reasons. First, it affirms that angels can and do function as God's soldiers, and in the ongoing troubles Jesus was having on earth, there was an ever-present option to simply call out the troops. But Jesus knew his struggle was not against either Jewish leaders or Roman imperialists. The showdown was with Satan himself, and it was not to be won on this occasion with an armed nighttime struggle in a garden.

The context for this cosmic showdown rests in the fact that notwithstanding an extensive body of theological thought and Old Testament scriptures that existed at the time of Jesus' birth, there was no accurate roadmap to redemption that was available to humanity. Jesus granted access to Heaven by filling in theological gaps, correcting theological errors, and explaining in plain terms what a person must do to be saved. Anyone who heard Jesus' teachings and truly believed and followed them would be allowed to enter Heaven.

However, the dilemma was that at the end of his ministry, Satan's work had caused few to believe that Jesus was the Messiah. Knowing this, Jesus was also aware that if his disciples had engaged in an armed conflict in the Garden of Gethsemane, they would likely have been overwhelmed by superior military might, and in death, they would have been regarded as simply another band of rebels. If angels had come down from Heaven and rescued Jesus, there would have essentially been a non-event. Either way, Jesus' Gospel would have been ignored and forgotten, and his entire mission would have been frustrated.

Satan needed Jesus to die in that garden, because having failed to defeat Jesus with temptation, betrayal, cruelty and other evil methods, Satan was left with only one weapon remaining in his arsenal. That was to kill Jesus physically, and thereby demonstrate Jesus' mortality and the invalidity of his teachings. For his part, Jesus knew he had to die a physical death so that he could overcome it, and by his actions declare to the world that Satan did everything to try to defeat him. He tempted him, he led others to lie about him, betray him and every other evil thing there is. But in the end when all that was left was for Satan to kill Jesus' physical body, even that couldn't prevail over God's might! Satan took his best shot and that wasn't good enough, so people should believe that Jesus brought us the truth.

Thus, Jesus couldn't die a quick, obscure death at the point of a blade. He had to position himself to have not only a notorious martyr's death, but also one that would allow Satan to throw everything he had at the Son of God. It was only by proving decisively his invincibility through death and resurrection that Jesus could establish definitively for the sake of any concerned onlookers that God's power on earth was supreme. From that point forward, every Christian and would-be Christian who learned of the resurrection would be satisfied of the legitimacy and credibility of the teachings of Jesus, as well as the fact that if they followed those teachings, they would be welcomed into Heaven.

Providing humanity with a roadmap to Heaven was actually only incidental to Jesus' primary objective. Jesus' primary objective was to deliver to humanity explicit instructions for how individuals can play a meaningful role in restoring the dominance of God's goodness on earth. This role has at least three important requirements. The first is that the individual must love God with all his or her heart and soul. The second is that the individual must be a good person him or herself. Jesus went into great detail about what is expected in the way of both personal and social morality. By far, it is this requirement that receives the most attention by many Christians. The third requirement, which is to comfort, protect and empower the poor, is the most troublesome to most Christians, but it is of extreme importance because its purpose is to look after those who will ultimately become God's warrior-saints.

God's warrior-saints come from all segments of humanity. "...I beheld, and lo, a great multitude, which no man could number, of all nations and kindreds, and people, and tongues, stood before the throne, and before the Lamb, clothed with white robes, and palms in their hands." Revelation 7:9. Nevertheless, this book focuses on only one group – enslaved Africans and their descendants. This is because although poverty and oppression often immobilize many diverse populations, Africans of the diaspora have actively and continually resisted injustice from the first moment of contact with those who sought to enslave them. While not entirely unique, this population is particularly suited to examination of its engagement in spiritual warfare.

The long-term suffering of Africans in the diaspora has steeled their moral integrity and consequently served as a nagging challenge to Satan and the forces of evil to conquer their souls. In the chapters that follow, we will examine how Africans in the diaspora weathered spiritual storms and repeatedly emerged victorious over forces that do not want them as part of God's army.

Chapter Two

Children of God Holding On To Self-Image

Soldiers in almost any army are required to submit to an ongoing physical conditioning regimen because those who engage in physical combat must be physically tough. An enemy's only hope of overcoming a well-conditioned soldier is to inflict fatal or disabling physical injuries. Otherwise, a committed soldier will draw upon a deep well of stamina to fight on until either he is killed, or the enemy has been vanquished. The circumstances of a spiritual warrior are comparable, in that spiritual toughness can be overcome only through complete spiritual devastation.

Africans victimized by the institution of slavery were pulled involuntarily into spiritual warfare. Contrary to popular belief, Africans engaged in unceasing physical resistance to slavery until it was destroyed.[2] Our point of inquiry is whether they resisted on a spiritual level as warriors and held up under the attack. Africans had a strong spiritual connection to God even before they were introduced to plantation-style Christianity. Active relationships with the Creator were very much at the heart of life in traditional Africa.

...God is no stranger to African peoples, and in traditional life there are no atheists. This is summarized in an Ashanti proverb that 'No one shows a child the Supreme Being.' That means that everybody knows of God's existence almost by instinct, and even children know Him.[3]

Africa's spiritual power is palpable and ubiquitous to this day to visitors who are open to recognizing it for what it is. As spiritually powerful people, Africans became a prime target for Satan. As the architect of the institution of slavery, Satan unleashed upon Africans and their descendants a psychic/spiritual assault of such dimensions that it is virtually unparalleled in all of human history. This assault was designed to permanently disorient enslaved Africans by persuading them of their utter worthlessness and their lack of any obligation to a God who had at least forsaken them, and possibly even subjected them to unimaginable suffering, oppression and relentless misery. Isaiah foresaw tragedy for Africans when he prophesied:

So shall the king of Assyria lead away the Egyptians prisoners, and the Ethiopians captives, young and old, naked and barefoot, even with their buttocks uncovered to the shame of Egypt. And they shall be afraid and ashamed of Ethiopia their expectation, and of Egypt their glory. Isaiah 20: 4-6.

26

This fear and shame of Africa which was brought on by not just the Assyrians but also by others who later led Africans away as captives, has perhaps been more spiritually devastating to Africans of the diaspora than any aspect of the slave experience. But it is also a testament to the spiritual power of Africans that in spite of this centuries-long assault, they have survived not only physically and mentally, but they are widely regarded as one of the most "religious" or spiritually active populations on earth. While Satan failed to turn Africans against God, he nevertheless succeeded in many cases in turning Africans against themselves. To the extent that Africans bear the burden of self-hatred, they suffer a disability that prevents their full spiritual development. How can they be truly thankful to God, and embark upon full service to him if in the dark recesses of their hearts, minds and souls, they believe that they have somehow been cursed by the same God who is the focus of their daily prayers and worship?

The universally perceived "curse" of being an African was brilliantly engineered by Satan. As we examine how he did it, it is important to note at the outset that the term "racism" is inadequate to explain what happened, because it implies that the phenomenon was not particular and unique. The term "white supremacy" is a more precise description of what inspired

27

institutionalized white chauvinism on the one hand, and African self-hatred on the other. Use of that term requires the conscious acceptance of the fact that thoughts and manifestations of white supremacy are not limited to hooligans wearing white hoods and sheets. For example, in a bygone era when cool cats in Harlem conked their hair and their dates bleached their skin, they were acting out white supremacist notions that they had internalized, even though they were Africans.

White supremacist doctrine sometimes seems as though it has always been part of the human experience. Certainly, relatively benign racial biases and prejudices have long been present. However, destructive white supremacy as we know it has a reasonably identifiable historical starting point, and it marked a tragic, radical departure from the then long-established course of human relations. For centuries, Africa was not only respected, but venerated by the rest of the world – including Europe. The high quality of scholarship and learning that occurred at universities and mosques in the West African cities of Timbuktu and Djenne were widely known.[4]

In his groundbreaking book *Black Athena*, author Martin Bernal demonstrates with the highest quality scholarship that ancient Greece and early Rome owed - and paid - a huge debt of gratitude to Africa for the development of what has come to be known as "western civilization."[5]

Likewise, other scholars have demonstrated that in the areas of mathematics, astronomy, medicine, metallurgy, and more, ancient Africa was well ahead of ancient Europe, and this fact was clear to European travelers who observed African accomplishments.[6]

Nevertheless, there came a time when a need arose for white supremacist doctrine. Bernal noted:

>...[I]t is generally accepted that a more clear-cut racism grew up after 1650 and that this was greatly intensified by the increased colonization of North America, with its twin policies of extermination of the Native Americans and enslavement of Africans. Both these presented moral problems to Protestant societies, in which equality of all men before God, and personal liberty, were central values which could be eased only by strong racism.[7]

The idea that Africans were subhuman was not one that was advanced only by brutish slave traders as a way to silence critics. By the 19th century, slavery was so integral a part of western societies that God's continuing insistence through conscience that slavery was wrong required a full scale satanic counter-offensive. Bernal noted:

29

If Europeans were treating Blacks as badly as they did throughout the 19th century, Blacks had to be turned into animals or, at best, subhumans; the noble Caucasian was incapable of treating other full humans in such ways.[8]

White supremacy was elevated from the status of mere hypothesis to full-fledged scientific doctrine. Thus, scholars began to fill books and journals with analyses of the following kind:

> The Negro race...is marked by black complexion, crisped or woolly hair, compressed cranium and a flat nose. The projection of the lower parts of the face, and the thick lips, evidently approximate it to the monkey tribe; the hordes of which it consists have always remained in the most complete state of barbarism.[9]

The following "scholarship" was also very typical:

> The black variety is the lowest and lies at the bottom of the ladder. The animal character lent to its basic form imposes its destiny from the moment of conception. It never leaves the most restricted intellectual zones...If its faculties for thinking are mediocre or even nonexistent, it possesses in its desire and as a consequence in its will an intensity that is often terrible. Many of the senses are developed with a vigour unknown in the other two races; principally taste and smell. It is precisely in the greed for sensations that the most striking mark of its inferiority is found...[10]

30

Armed with conscience soothing strong convictions that such racist tripe was "scientific," whites from all social strata found acceptable some of the most horrific acts imaginable during the long period of enslavement of Africans.

An English traveler visiting the great plantations in the final years of slavery described African Americans who 'from the moment they are able to go afield in the picking season till they drop worn out in the grave in incessant labor, in all sorts of weather, at all seasons of the year without any change or relaxation than is furnished by sickness, without the smallest hope of any improvement either in their condition, in their food, or in their clothing indebted solely to the forebearance and good temper of the overseer for exemption from terrible physical suffering.' Even large-scale slave owners who directed their business managers to provide reasonable care for slaves nonetheless advocated harsh measures to maintain the highest level of production. 'They must be flogged as seldom as possible yet always when necessary,' wrote one.[11]

Satan had clearly taken full control of those who tolerated these conditions, and he certainly must have been delighted.

This makes it all the more remarkable that in the face of such horror, Africans never collectively decided to throw up their hands, and in the words of Job's wife, "curse God and die." Africans could maintain the mental and physical strength to endure only if they had the spiritual strength -even in the face of relentless, ubiquitous white supremacist doctrine -- to continue to regard themselves as children of God worthy of his mercy, and confident of God's promise to ultimately bring deliverance.

As noted, Africans arrived on the plantations fully equipped spiritually. Christianity became a vehicle for the expression of that spirituality. In Africa, spiritual power was drawn from communal dancing in a circle. Plantation Christian worship occurred in this way, and not coincidentally, prayers and songs were expressions of the Africans' predicament and determination to achieve liberation – even if that meant physical death.

> ...I'll lie in the grave and stretch out my arms;
> Lay this body down. I go to the judgment in the
> evening of the day, When I lay this body down;
> And my soul and your soul will meet in the day
> when I lay this body down...

Because physical death for Africans meant a continuation of life in the land of the ancestors, death was not a defeat. As worshipers clapped, danced and moved in a circle – or "ring shout," Christianity became highly Africanized and immediately transformed into a spiritual weapon that was directed not so much at the earthly oppressor, but squarely at Satan himself.

Hold your light Brother Robert – Hold your light.
Hold your light on Canaan's shore. What make
old Satan, for follow me so? Satan ain't got
nothin' for do with me. Hold your light on
Canaan's shore...

It is reasonably clear that notwithstanding the force-feeding of a corrupted version of Christianity by the slave masters, the Africans themselves were crystal clear about the true nature of God, and the fact that he was their ally in their struggles against evil.

> The folk' would sing an' pray and 'testify' an'
> clap they han's, jus' as if God was right there in
> the midst with them. He wasn't way off, up in the
> sky: He was a-seein' everybody an' a listen' to
> ever' word an' a-promisin' to 'let His love come
> down.' My people would be so burden' down
> with they trials an' tribulations, an' broken
> hearts, that I seen them break down an' cry like
> babies...Yes sir, there was no pretendin' in those
> prayer-meetin's. There was a livin' faith in a jus'
> God who would one day answer the cries of his
> poor black chillen an' deliver them from they
> enemies. But they never say a word to they white
> folks 'bout this kine of faith. [12]

It is remarkable that although enslaved Africans had been trained to think of God as a remote, invisible deity who resided in a distant realm, the quote above is evidence that the Africans had stubbornly and on their own established their own relationship with God, and through that relationship, correctly determined that, like oxygen, God is ubiquitous. Furthermore, and notwithstanding the slave master's corrupted interpretations of scriptures that supposedly urged slaves to honor their masters, God stands squarely on the side of the enslaved and oppressed, and can be counted on to liberate them from bondage.

Thus, Africans were emboldened and energized by a God that actively related to them and animated them during worship in ways that were completely foreign to their white oppressors. Each group observed the other with curiosity and bewilderment. Whites marveled at how lively slave worship sessions were. Africans were perplexed by the relatively somber, nearly dead religious rituals of the masters.

Although Africans were denied earthly weapons, they really didn't need them, because on some level they understood that they were fighting a force that was bigger, and more evil than the worst slave master they could imagine. Defeating this enemy required that, notwithstanding their lives of misery they not yield to the temptation to sink into a state of hatred, bitterness and resentment toward a God who Satan wanted Africans to believe was responsible for their plight. This became their fight, and their weapons (in the form of their cultural expression) were well within their control.

As a central element of African culture, music was used to preserve hope, love of God and faith in his commitment to deliverance.

> Oh I know the Lord, I know the Lord, I know the Lord has laid His hands on me. Oh I know the Lord, I know the Lord has laid His hands on me. Did ever you see the like before? I know the Lord has laid His hands on me. King Jesus preaching to the poor. I know the Lord has laid His hands on me.

Certainly Africans were comforted by their songs, but the spirituals were not merely feel-good harmonies. They also reflect the Africans' understanding that God was actively fighting the oppression that they endured, and that the enslaved Africans had not only the opportunity, but a duty to engage in earthly actions to assist that fight. Thus, more than a few of their songs were coded resistance anthems and instructions for runaways and rebels.

> "...Oh freedom, oh freedom, oh freedom over me. And before I'd be a slave, I'll be buried in my grave, and go home to my Lord and be free..."

"...When Israel was in Egypt's land; let my people go. Oppressed so hard they could not stand. Let my people go. Go down Moses. Way down in Egypt land. Tell ole Pharaoh, let my people go..."

"...Steal away, steal away, steal away to Jesus. Steal away, steal away home. I ain't got long to stay here..."

"...Swing low sweet chariot...I looked over Jordan and what did I see - Comin' for to carry me home - If you get there before I do, tell all my friends I'm coming too..."

This integration of spiritual affairs with earthly struggles is both remarkable and profound when considered against the backdrop of the practices of those Christians who draw a bright impenetrable line between religion and the practical issues of the world. Although there are Christians who have dutifully said their prayers and attended Sunday morning worship services, they don't really expect that God will actively and routinely intervene in their day-to-day activities. This has been particularly true of many white Christians. In their minds, Biblical miracles are the stuff of mythology and fantasy. So convinced are they of the impossibility of the "supernatural," that many white

Christians become obsessed with developing theories that provide "rational" explanations for the miracles that occurred in the Bible. Not so the African. Africans have been less inclined to believe in coincidence. If a relative is ill and not expected to live, an unexpected recovery is not attributed to luck or a doctor's sudden inspiration. God did it. Even if the doctor attempted a novel procedure that on this occasion proved successful, God simply used the doctor as a medium.

Not only have Africans accepted God's direct intervention into earthly affairs as a reality, they have also been less inclined to believe that Christians should be passive bystanders in the contest between God and Satan. In 1822, Denmark Vesey, a former slave who had purchased his own freedom, became convinced that God wanted him to literally go to war against the institution of slavery. Using the African Methodist Episcopal (AME) Church as his base he organized 9,000 slaves into a rebel army and assembled an arsenal of guns, pikes and daggers that were to be used to kill the white population of Charleston, South Carolina. After burning the city, the Africans were to escape by ship to Haiti or Africa.

In his position as class leader in biblical discussion with the enslaved AME members, Vesey found in the Christian Scriptures, as did the black civil rights leaders of the 1960s, a moral imperative for radical social change. He was enabled to preach an apocalyptic rhetoric that made powerless men willing to fight for their freedom.[13]

Vesey was personally convinced that notwithstanding the violent nature of his plans, his mission was a holy one. His response to a doubter was simply: "The Lord has commanded it."[14] But Vesey's plan was betrayed by informants, and he and 77 of his comrades were executed before they could launch their attacks.

Nat Turner was similarly convinced of the need for a violent cleansing of a world that embraced slavery. He succeeded in carrying out a two day campaign that involved the use of axes, guns and assorted blunt instruments to kill white men, women and children – some of whom were in their beds when they were bludgeoned to death. Turner's grisly description of these killings in his "confession" chronicled by lawyer Thomas R. Gray might give pause to many. But before he is finally judged, it is worth noting the striking resemblance between Turner's circumstances and those encountered by figures in the Old Testament who led crusades that resulted in large-scale mass killings. The targets of Turner's violence were members of a society that was so saturated with evil that routine beatings and rapes of an enslaved population were not only tolerated, but in a very twisted way regarded as the will of God. In much the same way that Satanic populations were physically purged in the Old Testament, Nat Turner set out to rid God's creation of persons who, from his perspective, were so dominated by Satanic impulses that they were beyond redemption.

We may never know whether Nat Turner was simply a psychopath, or whether he was instead the divinely inspired avenger that he claimed to be. We do know that Turner was not simply acting out anti-white frustration. He was instead completely obsessed with a spiritual life that ultimately led him to embark upon a very bloody enterprise. In the years leading up to his rebellion, he was engaged in constant prayer, meditation and fasting. He had many visions and revelations. He described one of his visions in the following way:

> ...I saw white spirits and black spirits engaged in battle, and the sun was darkened - the thunder rolled in the heavens, and blood flowed in streams - and I heard a voice saying, 'Such is your luck, such you are called to see; and let it come rough or smooth, you must surely bear it.'

Was Turner witnessing cosmic combat between opposing spiritual troops as a preview of warfare that was coming to the earthly realm, and that was destined to consume him?

On still another occasion he had the following experience:

> I heard a loud noise in the heavens, and the Spirit instantly appeared to me and said the Serpent was loosened, and Christ had laid down the yoke he had borne for the sins of men, and that I should take it on and fight against the Serpent, for the time was fast approaching when the first should be last and the last should be first.

This particular vision is highly significant because it suggests that, in his mind, Turner's objective was not to kill white people for the sake of killing white people. It was instead to do battle with Satan (or "the Serpent") who was represented in physical form by his white targets. It is quite noteworthy that Turner, and many other enslaved Africans, had the ability to recognize, even in their most intense state of oppression, that their true enemies were not the flesh and blood beings who caused them so much earthly misery. This could happen only if the Africans retained enough sense of self-worth to believe themselves worthy of not only God's attention, but also his protection.

It was the belief that God would offer his protection that allowed everyday people who had never engaged in any political act to stand boldly and empty-handed before armed, hateful, racist southern law enforcement battalions during civil rights movement demonstrations. In response to profanity, racial epithets, and on occasion, physical attacks, these faithful African spiritual warriors offered prayers and a steely resolve that ultimately overcame the armed might of the state.

There is a thin line between faith and disbelief. However, if a person genuinely crosses the line into the realm of faith, then it becomes fairly easy to remain there, because God is at work constantly, and the faithful are able to recognize his deeds and remain in a constant state of awe at what he does on a daily basis. At the end of the day, faithful civil rights demonstrators might have found themselves in jail, but they did not regard their detention as a lapse in divine protection. Instead, they were able to rejoice that notwithstanding their having stared down the barrels of police firearms, God protected them from what would ordinarily have been certain death. A loving and protective God had made it possible for them to live and bear witness for him on yet another day.

Thus, for the oppressed African, who was completely faithful, it didn't matter how much Satan's worldly proxies insisted that the African was worthless and his plight hopeless. This African was witness to God's glory and God's assurance that his life had value. The spirit of the oppressed but enlightened African could not be broken.

Chapter Three

Extraordinary Faith - Extraordinary Power

The unwillingness to accept manifestations of God's presence and acts for what they are is perhaps the greatest obstacle to crossing the line into the realm of faith. This can be seen concretely in the age-old question by skeptics:

> "If God is so powerful, and he wants so desperately for us to believe in him, why doesn't he just show up on earth and reveal himself?"

The fact is that God did precisely that. He recognized the theological confusion that is present in the Old Testament scriptures, and he assumed human form, walked the earth and explained his doctrine in the most simple terms, even to the point of providing illustrative examples in the form of parables. There was nothing mysterious about Jesus. He did not serve up riddles or attempt to be enigmatic. It is only when Christians are unwilling to accept his teachings at face value that they begin to persuade themselves that Jesus was speaking in code.

For example, imagine the many Christians who comfort themselves by thinking: "He couldn't have been serious when he said we have to sell all that we have and give the proceeds to the poor." Thus, there are many contemporary Christians who wonder aloud why God does not return yet again to persuade the unbelievers. But God is not coming back again for that purpose because he is well aware of the futility of such an enterprise. Consider:

> And it came to pass, that the beggar died, and was carried by the angels into Abraham's bosom: the rich man also died and was buried: And in hell he lift up his eyes, being in torments, and seeth Abraham afar off, and Lazarus in his bosom...

(Luke 16:22-23)

> Then he said, I pray thee therefore, father that thou wouldest send [Lazarus] to my father's house. For I have five brethren; that he may testify unto them, lest they also come into this place of torment. Abraham saith unto him, They have Moses and the prophets; let them hear them. And he said, Nay, father Abraham: but if one went unto them from the dead, they will repent. And he said unto him, If they hear not Moses and the prophets, neither will they be persuaded, though one rose from the dead...

(Luke 16:27-31)

Thus, if skeptics are unprepared to listen to God Almighty who appeared in human form 2000 years ago, why would they be any more prepared to listen if he were to make a return visit?

The bottom line is that one must be prepared to accept God's word and earthly interventions for what they are, and in this regard, Africans have demonstrated rock solid consistency. This is a great mystery to many who have given thoughtful consideration to the high level of Africans' oppression that reaches back over five centuries. For them, logic compels the question: "How can these people maintain faith in a God that has not relieved such extensive suffering?"

Questions of this type bring into such stark relief the differences between the truly faithful and skeptics engaged in intellectual inquiry. The latter have no time for nurturing a relationship with God and experiencing his work over time. Instead, they want God to do a single dramatic "God thing" and eliminate oppression on a mass scale in a sudden visible way. In contrast, the former have an active, moment to moment relationship with God. They speak with him constantly and ask for and receive small interventions several times each day that cause them to not only marvel at God's grace, but to grow in their faith even more.

Consider that a hypothetical intellectual skeptic might observe an enslaved African laboring in the fields under the lash, and conclude that God has surely abandoned that wretched soul. At the same time, that same enslaved African is praising God as she reflects on the fact that a deal between planters that would have resulted in the sale of her infant son to another plantation fell through this morning, and she will get to keep her baby after all. This was an answered prayer, and this African's heart is light and filled with praise, gratitude and wonder, notwithstanding the back-breaking toil she is forced to endure.

Even though the intellectual will chalk the collapsed slave sale up to good luck or coincidence, for the faithful, such things do not exist, because everything that happens on earth is the product of the deliberate effort of God, man or the Devil. On this occasion, and for this African, there is no other explanation than that God killed the deal, because neither Satan nor the men involved in the attempted sale wanted the deal to fall through.

Non-believers reject the notion that everything that happens in life is the result of the deliberate effort of God, the Devil or an earthly being. On those occasions when an occurrence cannot be attributed to the actions of an earthly force or earthly being, the non-believer will declare: "It just happened." The strange irony here is that atheists, who insist that there is a material cause and explanation for everything, essentially rely on blind – almost religious - faith that they are correct. They will say: "The universe came into existence through a big bang. We don't know how the big bang was ignited, but there must be a material explanation for it."

When challenged to explain the origins of that "matter" that came together to cause "the big bang," the atheist retreats into defensive counter-attack: "If you believe there is a God, prove that he exists." This question generally marks the beginning of the atheist's intellectually dishonest debate posture. The same atheist who poses that question is prepared to accept – often on faith alone – that oxygen exists. The belief in oxygen is rarely based on physical, direct observation, but rather on its manifestations. The atheist is able to breathe and fire can burn, so they readily conclude that oxygen must exist – even though the average person is unable to see it with the naked eye.

Nevertheless, when the believer responds to the atheist's demand to "prove that God exists" with references to the impeccable design of nature's ecological balance, the extraordinary intricacy of the reproductive processes of living things, the fact that in all of their brilliance, human beings have been unable to create a soul-possessing human being in a laboratory, the atheist shrugs off such evidence as "unscientific."

It is highly ironic – and even a bit disturbing – that when presented with mysteries for which even science has been unable to find answers, the atheist will respond that there are numerous potential answers, and that atheists have *faith* that the materially-based solution will be found. Furthermore, they are prepared to conclude without conclusive proof, but essentially on the basis of personal conviction alone, that when the answer to the mystery is discovered, it will not involve a supreme being. The possibility of God is definitively and absolutely rejected notwithstanding the fact that the scientific approach demands a certain humility, an acknowledgment that humans do not yet know all things, and a general openness to all possibilities.

We have taken here a few gratuitous shots at atheists, but many must be given credit for at least wrestling with the most difficult spiritual questions. As part of their work, they often study religious texts thoroughly and actively engage in spirited debates with believers.

Contrast them with an even larger group that goes to great lengths to avoid even passing thoughts and conversations about religion. They may label themselves as "agnostic" or members of congregations that follow certain religious traditions, but which are at the same time "secular." These individuals labor under the crippling disability of fear. For them, the idea of an all-powerful, all-knowing supreme being who sits in judgment is so staggering - so mind blowing, that they would rather remain blissfully ignorant, and simply make their way through life without having to be accountable to a God who might look with disfavor on certain aspects of their lives. For still others, the fear is not of an unknown God, but instead a fear of how they will be perceived by those on earth. After all, it is only the uneducated and the unsophisticated who cling to religious myths, and the doubters certainly don't want to be lumped in with the ignorant rabble.

It is a near-universal absence of fear of spiritual matters that distinguishes Africans. No matter how daunting the concept of an eternal, almighty God may be for many, from the perspective of those who suffer under actual or perceived oppression, the more powerful God is the better. These individuals are less concerned about how they will be judged after death than they are with the prospect of having a heavenly ally who can stand with them against earthly forces that cause them problems in the here and now. Likewise, in African communities in the Diaspora, there is no embarrassment about having a relationship with God. In fact, the culture is such that having a connection to God is a badge of honor that is worn with great pride.

Africans' lack of fear of spiritual matters has been repeatedly translated into fearless confrontation with earthly perils. It is remarkable enough that during the 19th and early 20th centuries, in the most rural regions of the deep U.S. south, Africans would defend, or prepare to defend their homes against the Klan and night riders with prayers and rifles. However, it is even more amazing that during the Civil Rights Movement, Africans fearlessly faced growling police dogs, bloodthirsty white mobs, and antagonistic government authorities without guns and without flinching. These confrontations were routinely preceded by prayer sessions and spirited singing. In fact, it was not uncommon for these practices to carry over into the demonstrations themselves.

There are so many incidents of this kind in the history of the African diaspora that the frequently repeated suggestion - even within the African community itself - that Africans are afraid to fight for justice, collapses immediately under the weight of the historical evidence. This unfounded idea is reflected most famously in a composition by The Last Poets titled: "Niggers Are Scared of Revolution." But what becomes apparent to anyone who spends any significant amount of time discussing the struggle for justice with Africans is that they are not at all afraid. They are however circumspect and cautious. Their heartfelt conviction that God stands with them always as they seek that which is right does not lead them to embrace foolhardy protest plans, or even safe strategies that are unlikely to succeed. However, upon the appearance of even the slightest evidence that a strategy or tactic has good prospects for a positive, productive outcome, Africans will gravitate toward it without hesitation, and pursue it with maximum zeal. This was clearly demonstrated when nearly 100% of African voters supported President Barack Obama's candidacy in 2008.

Excerpts of recorded sermons of President Obama's then pastor, Reverend Jeremiah Wright were distorted and manipulated by political foes and the media into politically damaging weapons against what was to become America's first black President. Wright's comments were prophetic truth emanating from a highly respected theologian - and many Africans knew that to be so. Consequently, under different circumstances, President Obama's eventual decision to distance himself from Wright would have been immediately condemned by Africans. Within the African community, a pastor might be severely criticized by his own flock, but if he is attacked by the white power structure he is to be defended and supported at all costs.

However, many Africans believed that God was using Obama to bring about a racial breakthrough. In the scriptures, God had frequently used imperfect individuals to do his will on earth. Obama was clearly imperfect in the eyes of many because he not only rejected his pastor, but he also pursued a political agenda that all but ignored the African World and pandered to the corporate establishment and white voters.

Nevertheless, the very confusing dilemma of whether to side with Wright or Obama was resolved through faith that God was at work within the campaign, and even Reverend Wright should not derail the Obama train. Without mass meetings, planning sessions or e-mail alerts, Africans throughout the U.S. quietly, intuitively and shrewdly muted any criticism of the candidate, and successfully fought with a vengeance for his eventual election.

Given that President Obama has, as of the date of this writing, done little more than dutifully maintain a U.S. economic and political empire that is dialectically opposed to the revolutionary resistance of the oppressed, it is unlikely that he will be a liberating force in the political/economic realm. But through the highly visible presence of a black family in the White House for anywhere from four to eight years, he may yet have a profound social impact - particularly on children of all colors who may never acquire notions that Africans are incapable of holding the highest positions of executive leadership. The potential for this type of social rather than political gain was what motivated many Africans to give President Obama their support.

But whatever the eventual verdict on the Obama presidency, he is the manifestation of an extraordinary journey taken by enslaved Africans from the dank, filthy, crowded confines of slave ships, to decades of brutal oppression to exclusion and discrimination, to giving one of their own the position of head of state.

Nothing but faith could have provided a people with the necessary stamina and determination to not only endure such a history, but to also emerge from it with such a triumph.

Chapter Four

Warriors Who Turn The Other Cheek

It is a pretty safe bet that there are white people who believe that if given the chance, Africans would attempt to get revenge for centuries of oppression by attacking every white person within reach. Dreamers of these dreams probably project their own would-be emotions on to the oppressed people in their midst. They think to themselves - on a subconscious, if not conscious level: "If I had been treated that way I would go after every white person who crossed my path." When these individuals fight ferociously against affirmative action, or the promotion of Africans to positions of corporate and government leadership, they are motivated by fear that once Africans have institutional authority, they will use it as a payback weapon against white subordinates.

The fact is that Africans have rarely (if ever) used the limited authority they have obtained to retaliate. More typical is the post-apartheid experience in South Africa where "truth and reconciliation" were the order of the day. Some militant voices within the African World frequently lament what they regard as

Africans' excessive kindness, and hair-trigger willingness to forgive. But even as they voice their frustration, these militant individuals know any calls for revenge against white oppressors will not resonate among the majority of the African population.

At first blush, it may seem counter-intuitive to suggest that non-retaliation is a lethal act of war. But when consideration is given to the nature of the contest between God and the Devil, it becomes a little more obvious why it is vital to God's campaign. Satan wins when there is hatred and alienation among members of the human family. Nothing makes that more likely than emotion-driven, resentment-fueled combat. Jesus' "turn the other cheek" admonition provided clear instructions on how to respond to Devil-instigated aggression, but it is nevertheless one of the most misinterpreted and misunderstood aspects of Jesus' teachings.

Historically, pacifists have latched on to the turn the other cheek directive as evidence that Jesus shared their absolutist non-violent philosophy. Still others have likewise presumed that Jesus established a hard line prohibition against retaliation of any kind. That interpretation has been the source of great confusion and despair for those who regard such a suggestion as not only illogical, but a prescription for humiliation. However, Africans have somehow come to understand the true meaning of this teaching intuitively if not intellectually, and their clarity on this point accounts to a significant degree for the manner in which they have engaged their enemies.

Jesus' instruction to turn the other cheek was not a comment on pacifism. After all, Jesus was an individual who used a whip of cords to chase merchants from the temple, and who instructed his disciples to arm themselves with swords. (Luke 22:35-38) Like most scriptural passages, the instruction is understood only if it is taken literally and in the full context of Jesus' broader comment. For that reason, Matthew 5:38-48 is quoted here in full:

> Ye have heard that it hath been said, An eye for an eye, and a tooth for a tooth: But I say unto you, that ye resist not evil; but whosoever shall smite thee on thy right cheek, turn to him the other also. And if any man will sue thee at law, and take away thy coat, let him have thy cloke also. And whosoever shall compel thee to go a mile, go with him twain. Give to him that asketh thee, and from him that would borrow of thee turn not thou away. Ye have heard that it hath been said, Thou shalt love thy neighbor, and hate thine enemy. But I say unto you, Love your enemies, bless them that curse you, and pray for them which despitefully use you and persecute you; That ye may be the children of your Father

which is in heaven; for he maketh his sun to rise on the evil and on the good, and sendeth rain on the just and on the unjust. For if ye love them which love you, what reward have ye? Do not even the publicans so? Be ye therefore perfect, even as your Father which is in heaven is perfect.

This is a lesson that does not require a search for hidden meanings or tortured interpretations. Jesus quite simply and literally is challenging Christians to respond to antagonism, injustice and bad conduct in exactly the same way that God does. The point is not for Christians to stand passively and endure beatings or facilitate robbery. It is for them to provide those who do evil deeds with continuing opportunities for redemption. When we as individuals commit sins, we ask God not only for forgiveness, but also for the opportunity to demonstrate that we will not repeat our errors. If we are genuinely contrite, on each and every occasion, God wipes the slate clean and gives us another chance.

Thus, if someone smacks us in the face, we always have the option of striking back, abandoning that person and writing them off as a lost cause. However, the almost certain consequence of that is that whatever evil that caused the assailant to attack will remain in that person only to surface yet again on another occasion and to the detriment of another victim. The God-like response is to: remain with that individual, make an effort to help him appreciate the harm that he has caused, urge him to reform his conduct, pray for his redemption, and then to give him another chance to have a positive relationship with us. In other words, we would offer up another cheek so that the individual would have the opportunity to kiss rather than punch it.

The human impulse is to regard this as the response of a wimp or a sucker. But it actually is the response of a warrior. Consider that the war that God wages against Satan revolves largely around the number of souls that can be won over to the side of goodness. Satan succeeds when angry frustrated people who throw unprovoked punches at others remain stuck in the muck of evil and resentment. The most devastating blows struck by God's army occur when his soldiers aggressively seek and achieve the redemption of sinners.

A victory is achieved for God when a litigant who wins his adversary's coat through an unjust verdict recognizes the shame of his greed only because the other party, by offering up all of his clothing, helps the sinner to see the stark absurdity and wickedness of depriving someone of the most basic necessities of life. There is rejoicing in Heaven when a person who compels a person to walk a mile repents because the victim forces his oppressor to think deeply about his misdeed by not leaving when given the chance, and walking another mile voluntarily. Would-be allies of Satan who cross over into the ranks of the blessed servants of the Lord give added momentum to the campaign to expand the kingdom of God "on earth as it is in heaven."

Africans' slow but steady climb from the very depths of degradation, oppression and humiliation has not been without healthy doses of militancy which has sometimes been violent. However these actions (and certainly the non-violent protests of the African community) have always been grounded in an abiding belief that white oppressors can and will be redeemed. No matter how much suffering Africans may endure, they always give their oppressors yet another chance to change their ways.

The irony (perhaps shame) is that the second chances Africans give are not always appreciated, or even recognized. Consider slavery. The enslavement of Africans and the genocide of indigenous nations of the Americas compete for the title of the greatest crime against humanity ever perpetrated. For their part, Africans have in a most Christian way repeatedly made known their willingness to forgive those who participated in slavery and those contemporary individuals and communities that have been the indirect beneficiaries of slavery's legacy. However, following God's example, the willingness to forgive has not been unconditional.

When it comes to forgiveness, God does not gratuitously hand out pardons. Jesus was quite specific and quite clear that human beings are not expected to behave in ways that are any different from what would be expected of God himself. The sinner must first repent - genuinely and sincerely. It is only then that the sinner may expect forgiveness. Most significant is that forgiveness can be expected over and over again – provided that there is repentance for each sin. Jesus said no less is expected of men and women who are aggrieved on earth. In that spirit, Africans have repeatedly demanded and waited in vain for the repentance of their historical oppressors. Africans' expectation has been that repentance will be in the form of an official apology and/or monetary reparations for slavery's impact.

The longevity of Africans' mass movement for reparations is nothing less than remarkable when it is compared to the normal and expected behavior of individuals who are wronged. Save for those instances involving extraordinary individuals who possess extraordinary faith, the effort to offer the sinner an opportunity to repent and receive forgiveness is usually half-hearted at best. In most cases, when one who has committed a wrong declines or ignores an invitation to apologize and receive forgiveness, it is unlikely that additional invitations and opportunities will be extended. Nevertheless, when it comes to reparations, Africans have repeatedly begged and pleaded for responsible parties to take advantage of the opportunity for repentance that has been offered. Organizations have even been established to press the issue. But there seems to be no official move to pay reparations at any time in the foreseeable future – if ever.

The resistance to reparations has much to do with a reluctance by some to acknowledge that a sin was committed - and for a larger group that acknowledges the sin, there has been an unwillingness to accept responsibility for it. For many, the mere suggestion that they bear even the slightest responsibility for slavery is so traumatic that they suppress such thoughts, drown them in denial and salve consciences rubbed raw with soothing thoughts of President Obama and a mythical racially harmonious country that they like to believe that he leads.

Many black nationalist reparations activists are equally in denial about the nature of the struggle that they wage. They like to believe that they are engaged in militant action, but stripped to its very essence, the campaign for reparations is little more than a request - usually politely made - for those with power to show kindness and fairness to those without power by doing justice. If this is what the traditional reparations movement has become, and if it also shows no signs of prompting the repentance that is sought, then it has evolved into a movement that may no longer be squarely on point with Christian doctrine.

God is always ready to forgive sinners who repent and who beg forgiveness. But for those who don't, he is compelled by his war against evil to deal mercilessly with unrepentant sinners by abandoning them to the misery brought by evil forces, and ultimately to the fiery furnace of hell. For God to do otherwise would be to enable and encourage sin. Thus, if activists find that they are making no headway in their demands for repentance and reparations, then the time may have arrived for them to consider whether they are enabling the perpetuation of the impact of a historical crime against humanity by failing to radically change course.

There are a number of African organizations and movements that owe their genesis to their founders' conclusion that the forces of oppression in America will not be reformed or destroyed through logic and appeals to morality. These groups have adopted strategies that fall along the full continuum of the militancy spectrum, but all have gone beyond the idea of turning the other cheek. In most cases, they strive for independence, power and self-determination. The overall philosophical and ideological diversity of these movements has much to do with the complexity of Africans' struggle for liberation. This topic is addressed in Chapter Six.

Chapter Five

Armed Struggle and Spiritual Warfare

The question of whether use of weapons and guerrilla warfare can be employed in spiritual warfare, and whether acts of violence can be consistent with Christian principles generally has been the focus of more contemplation and discussion among Christians than it probably ever was by Jesus himself. Great moral questions are rooted in these concerns.

Without question, Jesus earned the title of "Prince of Peace." His life and teachings have been the inspiration for many pacifists. However, we have previously discussed why the scriptural passages that have been at least part of the foundation of pacifist beliefs may not support pacifist philosophy at all. Specifically, we have considered why the "turn the other cheek" admonition that is regarded by many as a rule against physical retaliation is instead an instruction in how to create opportunities for redemption and forgiveness. The declaration that "he who lives by the sword shall die by the sword" that is interpreted by many as a denunciation of the use of weapons was actually a specific instruction to disciples to refrain from interfering with the fulfillment of prophecy.

Pacifists are also challenged by several of Jesus' statements and actions. These include, among others: his militant, violent expulsion of merchants from the temple; his instruction to disciples to arm themselves with swords; and the presence of "zealots" or anti-imperialist guerrillas among the ranks of his disciples and followers.

The question of violence has been of great concern to religious leaders in Africa, the African diaspora and in America's southern hemisphere. In many countries that were deliberately underdeveloped by western capitalists, oppressive conditions for the poor have been so severe that it has seemed that the only logical, moral response has been armed resistance. Within these environments, theologians have considered the conditions of those they have served. Many, who have come to be known as proponents of "liberation theology" have concluded that armed struggle is not only acceptable, but in some cases a moral imperative.

On the other side of the fence, there are theologians who have concluded from their reading of scriptures that armed struggle is never acceptable. With respect to the work of his own movement, Martin Luther King, Jr. was certainly in that camp.

However, with all due respect to theologians who have formulated clear positions on this issue, Jesus provided no hard and fast rule on the question of armed struggle.

The mission of zealots, including (we presume) at least some in Jesus' entourage, was to end the occupation of Palestine by any and all means. They were known to stalk and kill Roman soldiers. Jesus never condemned nor praised this type of activity. It is almost as if it were completely irrelevant to his program and he spent little, if any, time thinking or speaking about it. He was quite clear that his "kingdom" was not of this world. Consequently, skirmishes and bloodletting by mortals was of relative insignificance to an individual who was engaged in a struggle to dominate the universe.

In the absence of clear guidance on the question of armed struggle, how then are Christians to view it? As in all things, they must pattern their own lives after the life Jesus led. He did not engage in armed struggle because it was unnecessary for the accomplishment of his mission. But there are hints that if physical conflict had been necessary for the fulfillment of prophecy, Jesus would not have hesitated to use force.

Specifically, as Jesus and the disciples were surrounded in the Garden of Gethsemane by a mob armed with swords and clubs, a member of Jesus' entourage drew a sword and attacked a member of the mob. In response, Jesus said: "Put up again thy sword into his place; for all they that take the sword shall perish with the sword. Thinkest thou that I cannot now pray to my Father, and he shall presently give me more than twelve legions of angels? But how then shall the scriptures be fulfilled, that thus it must be?"

It is noteworthy that Jesus did not instruct his follower to break his sword or to discard it altogether. He instead directs him to return it to its sheath thereby making it pretty clear that Jesus was not, as a matter of principle, opposed to weapons. He simply knew that armed resistance at that moment would frustrate the fulfillment of prophecy. There is also the obvious question of why, if Jesus were a pacifist in the contemporary sense of the word, he would allow one of his most intimate associates to carry a sword in the first place.

But perhaps more noteworthy is that Jesus implies that, under different circumstances, it would not be out of the question for him to call out a battalion of angels capable of wiping out the armed mob that surrounded him. So although Jesus had at his disposal a band of men prepared to fight, and legions of angels prepared to do likewise, he did not avail himself of those options

- not because of principle, but because in carrying out his part of God's plan, armed struggle was not on the agenda. What this means for those who entertain thoughts of armed struggle is that there must be the most careful introspection, prayer and analysis to determine whether under circumstances comparable to those faced by a modern would-be guerrilla, Jesus would have found it necessary to take up arms.

In the absence of a bright line rule on this question, we must emulate Jesus as best we can. Jesus refrained from armed resistance when he recognized that such would prevent the fulfillment of prophecy. We too must analyze on a case-by-case basis whether armed struggle is essential to the mission that Jesus spelled out for us. More to the point is the question of whether we can carry out that mission without engaging in violence. Jesus was quite clear about our mission. We are first to love God. Second, we are to love our neighbors as we love ourselves. As to the second element of the mission, Jesus said we are expected to: feed the hungry, clothe the naked, and to visit the sick and those who are in prison. Waging armed struggle is not found in those directions. However, Jesus is quite clear about the fact that we are to let nothing prevent us from completing our mission.

Thus, if in the course of trying to praise God or love our neighbors by satisfying their material needs we encounter resistance that can only be overcome with an armed response, it is possible that such may be justified in God's eyes. Few question the morality of Africans in the deep south taking up arms to defend themselves against night riders and the Klan. Likewise, when the Black Panther Party used rifles to defend the black community from brutal, racist police, it was clearly a justifiable response. Similarly, armed struggle to destroy colonialism and apartheid in Africa were morally just.

But use of violence is dangerous moral ground to tread because of the possibility that those who are on the receiving end of an armed response may well be "neighbors" who God expects us to serve and not wound; or sinners who, despite their offending ways, should receive opportunities for redemption through our willingness to turn the other cheek, and offer them yet another opportunity to treat us with respect.

On the other hand, the resistance to our holy mission may be the manifestation of satanic evil, and God may expect us to obliterate it. There are more questions than answers presented by issues like this, and they can only be answered by direct communication with God through prayer and the very best efforts to objectively determine how Jesus might respond under identical circumstances.

An examination of the history of Africans' struggle in America shows that they have navigated this terrain quite successfully. If Africans in America had chosen to engage in constant bloodthirsty violent retaliation, most reasonable people would have understood that reaction in the context of the brutal oppression that Africans have been forced to endure. But instead, Africans' resistance has been measured, controlled, calculated and considered. In most cases, it has been tempered by Christian doctrine.

Africans' march toward justice has been steady and unwavering with a resort to violence only when there have been circumstances that have threatened to derail progress and which could not be dealt with in any way other than by violent measures. In fact, a criticism of the African struggle in America is that when it has taken on a militant character there has been a failure to maintain and sustain the struggle on that level. To be concrete, in the wake of intolerable incidents of police brutality, urban "riots" have been of limited duration. These insurrections have not been transformed into organized guerrilla warfare.

Although there are many oppressive conditions in America that would make armed resistance morally acceptable, there are numerous practical reasons why spontaneous urban insurrection has not morphed into guerrilla warfare. Foremost among them is the absence of organization and ideological and strategic unity in African communities. But there is also a spiritually based reluctance to shed blood for the sake of venting anger.

Ultimately, African spiritual warriors will be best served by making the question of the morality of armed struggle as insignificant as it was for Jesus himself. If the primary concern is the accomplishment of God's mission, then that must be the overriding objective that must be achieved by any means necessary.

Chapter Six

For Africans, Politics and Religion Do Mix

The African fight for liberation is complicated by the fact that it has never been fought solely in the political arena. It has been multi-layered and has demanded the prosecution of multiple parallel struggles. In addition to seeking political power, Africans have had to struggle against white supremacy, while at the same time struggling for basic self-respect and dignity. Add to this the basic struggle for day-to-day survival. Africans themselves are not even aware of the many layers of struggle in which they are engaged.

Even activists in the community become confused. They may observe Africans deliberately and effectively struggling against white supremacy, and criticize the people's efforts because no identifiable political objectives are achieved. Consider the campaign for President Obama. African support for Obama was close to 100%. Yet, during the campaign, and certainly during the first 100 days of his presidency, there were more than a few African political activists and commentators who were critical not only of the fact that the new president's program was little different, and in some ways more conservative, than those of traditional white mainstream Democratic Party politicians, but also of the fact that criticism by the black community was muted.

But the millions of Africans who embraced Obama's candidacy and swept him into the presidency were not engaged in a political struggle, even though it occurred in the political arena. Instead, for Africans, the Obama campaign was part of an ongoing struggle to destroy white supremacy. For that limited purpose it was sufficient in the minds of many Africans for President Obama to simply win the election and demonstrate excellence in carrying out the standard agenda that the system imposes on every president. If he could do that, he would smash yet another lie about the capacity of Africans to function on the same level as whites. This is an important objective for Africans - not because they feel compelled to prove something to the white community - but because they feel the need to prove something to themselves (especially African children) in order to wipe out internalized, white supremacy-inspired inferiority complexes. Consequently, the Obama presidency did not have to result in political progress. It was however expected to change perceptions about what Africans can accomplish.

There was comparable confusion concerning the historic "Million Man March" in 1995. Minister Louis Farrakhan called for this massive manifestation for the sole purpose of having African men come together, connect with each other and atone for past behavior that may have been detrimental to the interests of their communities. Nevertheless, many activists and commentators were relentless in their criticism of the event because it lacked a political agenda and was "politically incorrect" because of its exclusion of women. Among critics, there was an unwillingness to accept that this event was a unique "happening" that was deliberately non-political, but nevertheless very important to Africans' intra-community struggle to regain self-respect, along with a shared sense of what constitutes a man's responsibilities.

Understanding that there are multiple layers of struggle in the African community is important because it not only leads to greater clarity and efficiency in the broad effort to achieve liberation, it also facilitates a genuine appreciation for just how complicated the oppressive circumstances of the African diaspora are. Other communities that fight only a single enemy concerning only a discrete problem can afford the luxury of a materialist, secular approach. Africans are so overwhelmed by the extent and enormity of their challenges, that they instinctively call upon God for assistance - for *every* fight that they wage. This practice is so much a part of Africans' culture that they turn to God even for those challenges where failure does not portend grave consequences.

This connection with God that reaches into almost every aspect of the lives of many Africans can run headlong into conflict with the programs of those activists who have been schooled (or who have schooled themselves) in political ideologies that were created or refined outside of African culture. For example, Karl Marx may have concluded that religion was the opiate of the masses after making specific observations of the role that churches played in the oppression of 19th century European workers, but this did not speak to the liberating role that religion played for Africans who were led by Nat Turner, Martin Luther King, Jr., Elijah Muhammad, Malcolm X, and many other religious leaders who regarded God as a champion of the oppressed.

Much has been written about liberation theology in the African community and the thoughts and deeds of the many great leaders who have embraced it either consciously or intuitively.

However, some - if not most - of these leaders would not have succeeded if the people themselves had not embraced them. These leaders (largely Christian and Muslim ministers) were enthusiastic about blending religion with politics.

More fascinating than African leaders are the clashes that the masses of spiritually committed Africans have had with African Marxists, Leninists, Trotzkyists, Maoists and even representatives of the Democratic and Republican Parties who have come into African communities with rhetoric that in the extreme urges the complete rejection of religion, or which instead more moderately suggests that there simply be a separation of religion from politics. The African community's reaction to these purely materialist, secular political ideas is rarely enthusiastic. Increasingly activists have learned that they dare not disregard the spiritual orientation and commitment of Africans if they are to have any hope of success in their communities. This in itself represents a victory by countless unknown everyday Africans in the realm of spiritual warfare.

As to this point, one of the most astute secular political leaders to emerge from the African diaspora was Kwame Ture, who was more widely known by the name Stokely Carmichael. Ture became famous for his work with the Student Non-Violent

Coordinating Committee during the Civil Rights Movement, but he spent far more time living and working in Africa, and at the same time traveling the world on behalf of the All-African People's Revolutionary Party urging Africans in the diaspora to make Africa the primary focus of their political agenda.

Ture concluded that the source of African people's oppression and exploitation throughout the world is the capitalist system and that the liberation of Africans around the globe will occur when the African continent has a single socialist government and economy that can fight for and sustain both the continent's population and its diaspora. His socialist plans for Africa forced him to grapple with certain socialist dogma that advocated atheism. Ture ultimately rejected such notions opting instead for the political analyses of Africans - specifically Kwame Nkrumah and Sekou Toure, whose ideas were socialist, and at the same time compatible with the spiritual commitment of Africa's people. For Ture, this was the only obvious option. He said:

Now, it goes without saying that one does not spend an adult lifetime organizing black folk without paying some considerable attention to the soul, as it were, engaging the spiritual. I certainly learned that in Mississippi. In Africa, we, of necessity, organize in Christian, Muslim and traditional communities. We respect all religions and all faiths.[15]

For Ture, the accommodation of religion within a political framework was not merely for the sake of expediency. He was very much the product of the African World that he sought to organize.

I've never been particularly sanctimonious, or what folks in the South call 'plu-pious.' But I am a religious man. As you've seen, I come from a family and a community of faith, a circumstance that has profoundly affected my personality and at one point my political allegiances. I strongly believe, for instance, that the strength to survive and continue working to this point comes in significant ways from sources outside myself. A great part of which, I'm convinced, has been the constant prayers of a great number of people of different faiths.[16]

It is indeed the power that has flowed from prayer and spiritual commitment that has made the critical difference for Africans politically. It has been a steely resolve inspired by the knowledge that no force on earth can defeat almighty God that has inspired Africans at every level to stare straight into the eyes of overwhelming hostile power and unflinchingly resist - with success.

God-inspired fearless confidence has occasionally been seen not only in African religious leaders, but in African political leaders as well. In his book *An Unbroken Agony*, Randall Robinson provides a detailed and highly disturbing account of how France and the United States, through their combined diplomatic, economic and military might, executed the 2004 kidnapping of Jean-Bertrand Aristide, Haiti's democratically-elected president.

The only thing more remarkable than Robinson's account of the vicious, criminal, unscrupulous actions of the western governments is the calm and grace of Aristide for the duration of the protracted episode. This calmness was likely rooted in faith, because Aristide, a former Catholic priest, was no ordinary hack politician. He truly understood God's power and this can be seen in the way that he connected effortlessly with God's people - the poor. In the book, Robinson wrote:

"Of all the public Christians I have known personally, Aristide led a life that emulated the implacable Christ whose sympathies for the poor Aristide had since childhood taken deeply to heart."[17]

Robinson went on to report:

"Driving in the [Haitian] countryside, however, I came to appreciate emotionally for the first time how widespread and painful Haiti's poverty is, and that the color of that poverty was all but exclusively black."

Robinson quoted a poor Haitian elder he encountered during his journey:

'The president [Aristide] is our hope...He and we are the same...Not just here on the outside' touching the dark skin on his arm, 'but here on the inside,' his hand again placed over his heart.[18]

It took a very special man to inspire that type of reaction, and Robinson's report of what Aristide said in response to the question "What is God?" helps us understand just how special he is. In *An Unbroken Agony*, Robinson quotes Aristide as saying:

First of all, God is love. That means that wherever there is love, true love, with kindness and compassion and honor and respect, God will be there. And God's goodness and mercy will be there. At the same time, God is all around us, and more importantly, within us. And so, each time you observe an act of kindness, an act of compassion and consideration, an act of mercy or justice, no matter how large, no matter how small, that is a manifestation of God. These are all manifestations of the God within us - proof of the divine spark that is within us all. And acts of kindness and mercy all around the world combine to create the Goodness and Mercy that is God - on a much larger and more dramatic scale.

It is the obvious spiritual clarity and commitment of Aristide that helps to answer the otherwise baffling question of why large, powerful western governments would hatch such an elaborate plan and dedicate such considerable resources to the kidnapping of a physically diminutive, soft-spoken social reformer. Certainly he had irritated French leaders with his demands for financial restitution for illegal economic embargoes during early Haitian history. Aristide had also become something of a thorn in the side of the Haitian elite families. But drastic actions such as assassinations and kidnappings of heads of state are rarely ventured unless there is the perception that the targeted leader poses a serious, imminent threat to corporate profits or western geo-political advantage.

In some ways, Aristide was a threat to western material interests, but the reaction to him as a leader was more likely the vicious visceral reaction of evil forces to the "divine spark" that resided within this humble leader of a suffering little country. This merits serious attention because when it comes to anti-imperialist rhetoric, Aristide was not alone among leaders of underdeveloped countries. Some of these leaders spoke in terms that were far more bellicose and militant. In some cases they would even be inclined to engage in military action against the western powers if they were sufficiently satisfied of their chances for success. However, evil forces consistently distinguish ordinary opposition from that which is touched by God. Evil's most fierce attacks are reserved for those who pose the most lethal threat to the Devil's plans.

Consider that it was not only Aristide who was the focal point for an attack by Satan. His entire nation was targeted. When Haiti was literally destroyed by the earthquake of January, 2010, many rushed to blame the saintly people of that poor country and God himself for the disaster. Evangelist Pat Robertson said:

> [Black Haitians] were under the heel of the French, you know Napoleon the third and whatever. And they got together and swore a pact to the devil. They said 'We will serve you if you will get us free from the prince.' True story. And so the devil said, 'OK it's a deal.' And they kicked the French out. The Haitians revolted and got themselves free. But ever since they have been cursed by one thing after another.

82

The illogic of this is remarkable. From cover to cover of the Bible, God pledges to protect the poor and to liberate the oppressed. So if we are to accept Robertson's analysis, Haitians resisting oppression and slavery struck a deal with Satan to do God's work!

But it becomes all too easy to understand why Satan chose to destroy Haiti with an earthquake when we look at how both the people of Haiti - and God - reacted. Amidst mountains of rubble and death, the Haitians prayed and sang spirituals - for weeks. When Haitians who had been buried beneath rubble for a week or more were rescued, they emerged smiling and explaining that they had been sustained by prayer. These survival incidents could only have been miracles by God himself.

It was from these spiritual people that Aristide emerged, and he was actually not unique. Like every other aspect of life, politics as practiced by Africans is permeated by spirituality. Nevertheless, as noted earlier there have been numerous African political actors, and non-African political actors with African constituencies who have adopted secular ideologies of European origin and have run head-long into African spirituality. When this has happened, not unexpectedly, God has ultimately prevailed.

In 1979, a popular uprising on the tiny Caribbean island of Grenada led to the installation of a government that included members who purportedly adhered to Marxist-Leninist ideology. Marxism-Leninism, according to many of its adherents, does not incorporate religion. Nevertheless, Grenada's leaders understood intuitively if not intellectually that the spirituality of the overwhelmingly African population had to be accommodated. Maurice Bishop, the Prime Minister, explained during a speech:

...[T]he church has received the fullest cooperation, respect and noninterference from our government and revolution. Our record has been and our position today continues to be one of total cooperation: duty-free concessions; help in fixing church property; help in fixing church schools; full and prompt payment of government grants to church schools; regular meetings between the prime minister and church leaders on a wide range of issues when the discussions have been frank, free, cordial, and constructive; total freedom of religious worship; complete support for religious education in all schools and so on. We have cooperated in this way because we recognize and respect the people's desire for moral and spiritual upliftment. This is why we have not attempted to interfere with the church in its function of ministering to the moral and spiritual needs of our people.[19]

The depth and power of African spirituality was not lost on the leader of another Caribbean island during the same decade. Michael Manley, a secular politician and Jamaica's Prime Minister, understood early on that his success required the perception of harmony between his political program and the Bible-based faith of Rastafari, an essentially Christian movement that regards Ethiopian emperor Haile Selassie as the second coming of Christ.

> Manley's awesome popularity in 1972 was based on a charisma that drew on Rastafarian imagery, a watered-down black power appeal, and an intelligent and persuasive oratory adaptable to the streets or a boardroom. He adopted the name Joshua and brandished the 'Rod of Correction,' a cane given to him by Haile Selassie himself.[20]

Even in Cuba, which pursued perhaps the most doctrinaire approach to Marxism-Leninism in the Caribbean, it was not possible for the government to insist on a purely secular society. African culture and African spirituality in Cuba are very strong, and the government was unable to completely suppress religious practices in that country. With the passage of time, Cuba has become even more tolerant of religion.

Many more examples could be given of the connection between spirituality and African politics, but such is unnecessary for even the most casual observer of movement history in the African World. For Africans, spirituality is an indispensable element of political work. But it also provides Africans with a tremendous political advantage. This is because regardless of the actions of earthly oppressors and the measures they use to restrain and constrain African populations, a strong spiritual orientation of an oppressed group can be liberating in and of itself.

To be more specific, when a person literally lives with the belief that detention, torture and even the killing of the human body are nothing when compared to the catastrophic consequences of the loss and destruction of the immortal soul, that alone alters the relationship between the oppressed individual and his or her oppressor. The power of the oppressor comes from the capacity to inflict physical harm on the oppressed, and a willingness to use the threat of such punishment to intimidate and coerce. If the oppressed fear physical consequences, they will conform their conduct to the wishes of the oppressor in order to avoid physical punishment.

However, if the oppressed fear God more than mortal enemies, and if they are also convinced of the legitimacy of the divine promise that the souls of those who willingly sacrifice their lives for God's kingdom will be saved for eternity, the oppressor loses all power and influence over those he seeks to oppress. For generations now, many Africans who have sought political change have done so without regard for the tactics of intimidation that have been used against them. Threats of jail and even lynching have been met with cries of: "Go ahead and kill me and I'll just go home to be with my sweet Jesus!" There is little that evil, oppressive forces can do to stop the political march of waves of determined Africans willing to die for the sake of their Lord and eternal life.

Chapter Seven

Spiritual Transformation Through Prophetic Witnessing

Many years ago, I penned the following verse:

> *You will not have truly won the war if, for fear of revenge you cannot lay down your sword and shield.*
>
> *Save the souls of the oppressors - Teach them the ways of the Lord - and when they gladly give love and seek justice, then you will have a real revolution.*

The poem was inspired by reflections on experiments in political revolution that have occurred in a number of countries throughout the world.. In some cases, popular revolutions have succeeded in seizing state power, and also ushering in fundamental changes that have positively impacted the social and economic conditions of the people. Nevertheless, there have been vanquished members of some overthrown regimes who have seethed with resentment in prison cells and in exile, and who have engaged in relentless efforts to subvert the revolution. The natural and expected consequence is that certain revolutionary governments have been forced to remain forever on guard to defend their gains. Ideally then, enemies of the revolution must be spiritually transformed so that they will abandon the cause of counter-revolution.

Saving souls is far more difficult than driving a dictator from power at the point of a rifle. It requires the channeling of God's love and power through prophetic witnessing, and a willingness to endure retaliation. Witnessing may not always involve the mere quoting of scripture in public places and testimony about God's goodness. In the tradition of Old Testament prophets and Jesus himself it more often requires "speaking truth to power" about moral and ethical failings that sinners least wish to discuss or even acknowledge. Historically, the fate of prophets and others who have dared walk this path has been torture and/or assassination.

For example, Jesus publicly and relentlessly described the ways in which religious leaders exhibited hypocrisy, arrogance and greed. The piety of these religious elders had led them to deeply suppress any guilt they may have felt about their moral failings, and when Jesus publicly "called them out" it triggered intense, violent emotions that ultimately fueled the movement for Jesus' crucifixion.

This point about the nature of prophetic witnessing must not be missed because the more popular idea that all one need do is stand on a street corner and proclaim God's glory provides an easy escape from true Christian responsibility. Even the most sinful hypocrites welcome public discussion about the Gospel - provided that it is discussed in the abstract. However, when a true witness chooses to point an accusatory prophetic finger at the hypocrite, then the stage has been set for a hostile, maybe even violent reaction.

Historical circumstances have made Africans in America not only victims, but prophetic witnesses to racial injustice. It is America's greatest sin. It is also the sin that America - especially white America- is most determined to deny. Nevertheless, at every historical turn, Africans have been a nagging, visible reminder that white supremacy is the cancerous sin of the nation that not only fails to go into remission, but which continues to metastasize into the very heart of the society. Unable to accept this reality, America lashes out at those who sound the alarm. Africans from David Walker to Frederick Douglass to Ida B. Wells to James Baldwin to millions of anonymous Africans have stood up and delivered a prophetic warning. In return, they have been targets for intense hostility. Martyrs like Medgar Evers and

Martin Luther King, Jr., have paid the ultimate price.

The blows that Satan lands in his campaign to preserve racial division are potentially demoralizing. However, African persistence has been fueled by prayer and a sense of shared suffering and a shared faith in the promise of divine deliverance. This faith, which has sustained a people through generations, has also lulled many Africans into a state of racial denial that is in many ways comparable to that which afflicts their counterparts in the white community.

Many white citizens maintain their racial denial by latching on to superficial evidence of racial progress and they comfort themselves with thoughts of a black President. These thoughts make it easy to ignore the racially disproportional prison populations, mortality statistics, school graduation rates, poverty data and numerous other indicators of continuing racial inequality. For their part, many Africans are in a state of racial denial- not about statistics that reflect systemic and institutional racial discrimination, but about the willingness and capacity of white members of society to reform their racial attitudes, beliefs and conduct.

Many Africans desperately want to believe that acts of interracial kindness by whites are evidence of racial transformation. They frown on any mention of racial injustice because of naive fears that white people who are attempting to mend fences will become frustrated and simply abandon their efforts at racial reconciliation. However, it actually takes little to demonstrate that the white community has not progressed nearly as far as deluded Africans would like to believe. Serious proposals for the fundamental restructuring of institutions in order to eliminate white privilege will instantaneously erase smiles from the faces of many presumably well-meaning whites.

There is a continuing place in humanity's development for prophetic witnessing about racial sins. But if it is to happen, it should have meaning and produce results. America's reality is that those who offer racial analysis to white audiences might just as well preach to an uninhabited wilderness. Even many members of the white community who are well-intentioned are unable to "get it" for many complicated reasons - foremost among them is a state of denial about the inescapable fact that to achieve racial justice, whites will have to surrender their privileged status.

Those deluded Africans who confuse interracial civility with genuine racial progress presume that interracial dialogue is sufficient. But those Africans whose prophetic racial witnessing has had the greatest impact have never been confused on this point. Many who know little about Dr. Martin Luther King, Jr. incorrectly believe that he got results solely through civil discourse. However, even at the dawn of his public life, Dr. King knew that race discussions alone with the white community were futile. He understood the necessity of forcing the sinners out of their comfort zones and making them take stock of their sins. Dr. King accomplished this through mass disruption.

Dr. King knew that the white community prized order and stability. His boycotts, pickets and demonstrations caused the de-stabilization of local economies and public spaces. The white community's desperation for a return to the status quo forced them to listen - seriously listen to what Dr. King had to say. He forced about as much racial progress as any one man and his movement can be expected to produce within such a limited period of time.

What now for those Africans who wish to resume prophetic witnessing on the issue of race? As successful as they were, Dr. King's tactics are no longer viable. In the decades since his death there have been numerous efforts by numerous diverse social movements to replicate the direct action tactics of the Civil Rights era. This has caused most law enforcement agencies to train and prepare themselves to efficiently and professionally handle mass public demonstrations. These manifestations are now so routine that they create no disruption or inconvenience of any kind for populations that need to be taken from their comfort zones in order for them to really hear and understand the messages communicated by demonstrators.

Identifying an approach that will cause inconvenience requires an evaluation of the society's vulnerabilities. In the early 1950s, Dr. King and his colleagues correctly determined that Montgomery, Alabama was vulnerable in the area of public transportation, and a bus boycott forced a racist white power structure to sit down and talk. In 21st century America, the country is vulnerable with respect to, among other things, its use of petroleum.

If Africans in America were able to control the flow of oil into the country, those who need to listen to prophetic witnessing about race would, in the hope of restoring access to oil, beg for the opportunity to hear the message. This is not a matter of theory or speculation. In recent years, an organization called the Movement to Emancipate the Niger Delta (MEND) has sabotaged oil pipelines in Nigeria and caused substantial oil profit losses. If nothing else, MEND has gotten the attention of the oil industry. Imagine then if Africa's people collectively owned the oil operations in Africa that are now owned by non-Africans. Africans everywhere in the world would then be able to dictate the terms for discussions about pretty much anything on their minds - including race relations- simply because they would be perceived to have connections to those who control a major oil supply. This is a dream that must become a reality, and it can be accomplished only through the diligent efforts of generations of Africans around the world to unite the African continent into a single socialist super state.

A new day has arrived and the forces that determine the fate of Africans in America are no longer local or even national. They are global and they demand a global strategy that can ultimately place Africans in a position to, through prophetic witnessing, save the souls of the oppressors, teach them the ways of the Lord, compel them to gladly give love and seek justice, and in the end create a real revolution.

Chapter Eight

African Spirituality Meets European Secularism

From the seventeenth through nineteenth centuries, efforts by countless Europeans to practice their faith were met with horrific persecution. Wars of a sort raged between Catholics and Protestants. Mennonites, Huguenots and various other sects were at various times targeted for attacks. Torture, detention and death were often the penalties for those who were unwilling to practice the "correct" religion. At the root of much of this was Europe's intolerance of diversity. Conformity and uniformity were hallmarks of European culture, and this likely accounts for what was then an ongoing battle among religious groups to administer official state religions.

In addition to inter-religious squabbling, the church also became an oppressive institutional force within European society. It often dominated government affairs and enriched itself at the expense of workers and the poor. There is little wonder that on the basis of what he observed in 19th century Europe, Karl Marx condemned religion.

European religious persecution is often cited as a motivating factor for those who fled Europe with hopes of establishing a new home in North America where religious tolerance would reign. As the U.S. constitution and the new country's governmental framework took shape, the white men who crafted them were heavily influenced by memories of Europe. Concepts such as the "separation of church and state" were designed specifically to safeguard the new nation from the plight of the lands from whence they or their recent ancestors had fled.

However, as years passed, government devices intended to protect religious freedom spawned other cultural patterns that have had a heavy impact on social dynamics in the United States. Specifically, religion became compartmentalized within many white communities. The idea of "church" was not abandoned, but it was consigned to Sunday mornings, and Sunday mornings only. In addition, spirituality - which is distinct from the church as an institution - was in many cases abandoned by those who had soured completely on the church as an institution, and who presumed that anything associated with it (including spirituality) was tainted and equally deserving of rejection.

One consequence of the drive for a secular government through the compartmentalization of religion was a drive for a secular society. All things spiritual were eliminated from all aspects of life - except the church. Art, athletics, literature, and most especially science were stripped of any elements that were non-material and that might in some way be regarded as "supernatural." Atheism became, over time, not only tolerated, but respected as a reasoned, sophisticated approach to life.

All of this is in direct conflict with the experiences, sensibilities and aspirations of Africans and other peoples who did not have the European experience. In Africa and in African communities in the diaspora, spirituality pervades every aspect of life. Athletes pray before, during and after games. Artists presume that their talents are God-given and they constantly express their gratitude to God for their blessings. As we have seen, God has a prominent place in the political thoughts and movements of Africans. However the most controversial tradition is probably the African World's integration of spirituality with science.

When European culture compartmentalized religion, it most certainly divorced it from science. As a consequence, the western world has developed a concept and definition of science that is unique, but nevertheless arrogantly regarded as the only reasonable scientific view. European science is entirely empirical. It is presumed that all natural phenomena are the result of natural causes. European science demands the limitation of scientific inquiry to that which is tangible, material and quantifiable.

This is unique because some non-European cultures approach science in a more humble, open, less constrained, intellectually honest way. Scientists from these cultures begin with the presumption that not all phenomena can be fully explained. This approach led Chinese scientists to identify and accept that within the human body, there is an intangible life force that they call "chi" that is situated in the lower abdomen. Chi flows through "meridians" to different parts of the body. Controlling the flow of chi for the purpose of healing is the purpose of acupuncture.

Notwithstanding the demonstrated success of acupuncture, there are many in the western science community who refuse to accept it as true medical science. They also cavalierly insist that chi is nothing more than bio-electric energy or adrenaline. They are very uncomfortable with the idea of an intangible, unexplainable force in the body, and rather than accept it, they prefer to forego the healing possibilities of acupuncture for persons whose illnesses might otherwise be ameliorated.

In a paper presented at the National Science Teachers Association convention in 1992, author Brian Murfin observed:

> Many persons believe that science as practiced by Africans, females and other cultures may hold the answers to some of the intractable problems western science has created. Molefi Asante, the leading proponent of Afrocentrism, states that 'Western science, with its notions of knowledge of phenomena for the sake of knowledge and its emphasis on technique and efficiency is not deep enough for our humanistic and spiritual viewpoint.' How ironic it is. Many Europeans view African culture as primitive while some Africans question the whole foundations of modern western science.[21]

Murfin went on to provide the following poignant quote from Asante:

> [For Africans] [t]he self is the center of the world, animating it, and making it living and personal. Neither materiality nor spirituality are illusory. This is why the idea in western science of progress is troubling. Progress for the west is not more knowledge, but more technique. How to do it faster, smoother, longer, louder and with

greater exploitation becomes the pass-key to a techno-scientific future. Progress in an Afrocentric manner is related to the development of human personality because we are the source of life for the material and the spiritual; when we become more conscious of ourselves we shall be advanced and make progress.

Western scientists' arrogance is not only limiting and sometimes self-defeating, it can also ironically contradict its own scientific method. Imagine one of those elaborate domino displays that are occasionally showcased on television variety programs. These are remarkable because the tipping of only one of these little blocks sets in motion the lightning-fast sequential fall of hundreds of other dominoes that tip over tiny buckets of water, cause small wheels to spin, ignite small flames and many other amazing special effects.

If a western scientist is asked to explain how the little bucket of water was emptied, he will examine the display and after momentary analysis conclude that it was turned over by domino number 562. If asked what caused domino 562 to fall, he will conclude that it was domino 561. This process can continue in like fashion until he reaches domino number one. If the display designer is not present, the scientist will conclude that some thing or someone tipped over domino one. Further, upon evaluation of the precision with which each domino was placed in order, the scientist will conclude that the display did not materialize as the result of random coincidences, but was instead the product of the design of an intelligent human.

Nevertheless, many scientists will examine the wonders of the universe, and explain the existence of life forms and other natural occurrences by the impact of pre-existing natural forces on conditions conducive to evolutionary development. The scientist is able, with empirical evidence of evolution, to work backwards to an explosion, or a single "big bang" caused by a mixture of random gases and elements that triggered a natural sequence of changes that culminated in the formation of the universe that we all inhabit.

However, unlike the scientific method that is used to explain the tipping of domino number one and the orderly sequence of the hundreds of other dominoes, some scientists are prepared to attribute the ignition of the big bang and the orderly process of evolution that followed to mere random coincidence. What's more, they are not even willing to consider as even a remote possibility that a supernatural force is responsible. This flatly contradicts conventional scientific method which does not allow any possible explanation for natural occurrences to be ruled out until it has been excluded definitively by testing and experimentation.

The unwillingness of western scientists to at least consider supernatural causes for natural phenomena is not only contradictory, but likely self-defeating. African science, which incorporates immaterial as well as material factors into its analyses, historically outpaced European science, and failed to dominate it long term only because of colonialism, the slave trade and general underdevelopment of the African continent. It was from Africa that the west learned how to create the smallpox vaccine and perform C-section births. Long before Europe had made comparable discoveries, Africans understood the solar system; discovered stars not visible to the naked eye; forged carbon steel in blast furnaces; conducted autopsies; and much more.[22]

> [Molefi] Asante also points out that recent discoveries related to energy, gravity, and quarks can be better explained using non-western ideas. He gave the example of the search for the smallest particle which has continued from atoms to electrons to quarks and the Afrocentric realization by some scientists that they may never find a discrete answer to this question.[23]

The dominance of European culture in not only science but other aspects of life in the African diaspora creates not only a dilemma, but a challenge for Africans wishing to express their spirituality. This overriding predicament represents one of the great historical accomplishments of Satan. The natural spiritual expressions of a very spiritual population have been effectively hamstrung by a dominant society that has little use for spirit-led lifestyles.

Africans have not been content to accept these circumstances. Understanding early on that as a minority population in the diaspora they were incapable of effecting a revolution in the culture of the societies in which they resided, they instead created their own spirit-based societies in the places where they lived. In his groundbreaking book *The Souls of Black Folk*, W.E.B. DuBois observed and chronicled this phenomenon. He wrote:

> The Negro church of today is the social center of Negro life in the United States, and the most characteristic expression of African character. Take a typical church in a small Virginia town: it is the 'First Baptist' - a roomy brick edifice seating five hundred or more persons, tastefully finished in Georgia pine, with a carpet, a small organ, and stained glass windows. Underneath is a large assembly room with benches. This

building is the central club-house of a community of a thousand or more Negroes. Various organizations meet here, - the church proper, the Sunday school, two or three insurance societies, women's societies, secret societies, and mass meetings of various kinds. Entertainments, suppers, and lectures are held beside the five or six regular weekly religious services. Considerable sums of money are collected and expended here, employment is found for the idle, strangers are introduced, news is disseminated and charity distributed. At the same time this social, intellectual and economic center is a religious center of great power. Depravity, Sin, Redemption, Heaven, Hell, and Damnation are preached twice a Sunday with much fervor, and revivals take place every year after the crops are laid by; and few indeed of the community have the hardihood to withstand conversion. Back of this more formal religion, the Church often stands as a real conserver of morals, a strengthener of family life, and the final authority on what is Good and Right.[24]

Thus, the church has been for the African a refuge from an irreligious dominant culture, and it appears that it will continue to be so for indeterminate years to come. It is within the church that an African can speak at length about the integration of God with science, art, athletics and everything else without fear or concern of being silenced. It is this which presents the

105

great irony. The rules established by the European community to protect itself from unwelcome religious speech and acts can also be useful to the African as a shield against the dominant irreligious culture.

The point of conflict then in the spiritual war is not with those who seek to maintain a legal framework that protects the society from a return to European-style religious oppression, but rather on a more fundamental level there is a struggle for cultural transformation. In other words, African spiritual warriors, through their practice and the consequent example that they set, have much to teach those with cultural traditions that manifest religious intolerance. Ultimately, the laws that protect religious freedom will become obsolete because of an emerging consensus that God is supreme and thoroughly integrated into every aspect of life - including those that have traditionally been regarded as fit only for secular treatment and consideration.

Chapter Nine

Capitalism: The Devil's System

One of many lessons taught by Jesus was that human beings cannot successfully serve God and "mammon" (i.e. riches obtained through greed). Repeatedly he emphasized that personal wealth has no place in the life of a servant of God. He said a camel has a better chance of getting through the eye of a needle than a rich man has of entering Heaven. He instructed rich followers to sell all of their possessions and place the proceeds into a common treasury used to satisfy the material needs of the poor.

In fact, the economics of his community of believers ensured that there were neither rich nor poor.

"And all that believed were together, and had all things common; And sold their possessions and goods, and parted them to all men, as every man had need." Acts 2: 44-45.

Centuries later, a materialist philosopher named Karl Marx was to be inspired by the example of early Christians, and his doctrine urged: "From each according to his abilities; to each according to his needs."

Nevertheless, the early Christians' practical, common-sense, moral approach to the use and possession of material wealth is regarded throughout the western industrialized world as "radical," "subversive," "dangerous," and unconscionable. It is in the area of economics that Satan has had one of his greatest successes. He has transformed in the minds of the majority that which is virtuous into evil; and that which is evil into virtue.

Capitalist culture regards traits such as individualism and greed as not only desirable, but essential to the proper functioning of society. Capitalist theory contemplates economic class divisions (i.e., chronic, permanent poverty for some) and periodic society-wide economic crisis as predictable and unavoidable features of a capitalist economy. These concepts and values are so deeply held and pervasive in western industrialized countries that anyone who questions them (much less challenges them) becomes the focal point for immediate visceral condemnation, ridicule and ostracism. How did this happen? Jesus certainly did not wish for us to live in this way.

When Satan unsuccessfully attempted to tempt Jesus in the wilderness with wealth and power, he did not make the Holy Redeemer his final target. The countless individuals who later turned their back on God in pursuit of mammon had their way paved by Satan, who understood that individuals who not only regard themselves as gods of a sort, but have the capacity to impose their will on others will certainly do so. Thus, in the industrialized west, very rich and powerful individuals and corporations have used their resources to not only persuade the mass population via popular culture, mass media, advertising and other means that the circumstances of the rich are acceptable, but that they also represent the ultimate in virtue and morality.

Many years ago, when the author spent a few months as a college undergraduate intern in the office of a U.S. Congressional representative, he had the opportunity to observe several advertising industry lobbyists attempt to dissuade the Congressman from pursuing passage of a bill that would disallow tax write-offs for the cost of alcoholic beverage advertising. The lobbyists reeled off a litany of benefits of advertising, including their claim that it was advertising that made it possible for them to market filtered as opposed to unfiltered cigarettes in underdeveloped countries.

The Congressman listened politely for a few minutes, but ultimately rose from his chair and in thunderous tones lambasted the advertising industry for creating artificial and harmful demand for big gas guzzling cars, unhealthy fast food, tobacco, and alcohol of course. He ordered the lobbyists out of his office and he slammed the door as they stumbled shell-shocked into the reception area. When one of the lobbyists finally regained his composure, he glared at young staff members who were having difficulty hiding their amusement and declared: "You know what the problem is? It's not with advertisers. It's with your generation! Your generation is not in the church. We're in the church. You know who goes to my church? Executives of AT&T and I.B.M.!" With that he took his leave.

The point of the story is that the wealthy and powerful frequently lay claim to God. They are often the picture of respectability. A silver-haired, distinguished gentleman dressed in a $3,000 suit might emerge from his Bentley and gently take the hand of his prim, expensively attired wife and enter an uptight WASPy Presbyterian church where they sing a hymn or two, and hear a ten minute sermon before retiring to their mansion to review their investments and relax before beginning another week of corporate activity that will have the effect of exploiting and possibly killing large numbers of people in poor domestic communities or in underdeveloped countries abroad.

It is the wealthy and the powerful who portray themselves as the virtuous counter to the evil "communists" who are determined to take away their money. Their Satan-inspired genius is seen in the way that they have not only cast themselves as the bulwark against evil, but in the way that they have also persuaded the "middle class" and even some of the domestic poor that they too have a stake in the preservation of this elite class and the economic system that sustains the rich.

Africans have not been immune to all of this. On a conscious level, they want to be a part of it. Africans - particularly low-income Africans - long for material possessions. They fantasize about having big houses, big cars, fancy clothes and so much money they can afford to throw fistfuls of it away.

This longing for things is particularly acute among the poor in the industrialized west because they are forced to live from day-to-day possessing nothing in a society where wealth possessed by others is not only visible but sometimes flaunted.

Compounding the tragedy of Africans' lust for material possessions is an ongoing industry that has as its sole objective the feeding of this hunger with bangles, beads and assorted glittering junk that Africans in poor communities consume ravenously. Nobody with real wealth would ever seriously consider buying grillz for their teeth, spinning rims for their tires, or sneakers that contain numerous features and special functions that have nothing to do with enhancing athletic performance. Nevertheless, for those who own nothing it seems logical that the lack of possessions is the variable that if changed would end their state of misery. Thus, some Africans who lack sufficient income to pay for food, shelter and other necessities will use an unexpected windfall to buy "bling."

Africans are notoriously gullible consumers. But in spite of Africans' failure to resist carefully designed, psychologically-rooted advertising and marketing campaigns, they have, as a community, continued without interruption to resist the internalization of capitalism's most evil principles. One of the most critical capitalist principles is individualism. A good capitalist ruthlessly looks out for self and self alone. When a capitalist succeeds in amassing a fortune, that individual receives all credit for this achievement. On the other hand, if a crime is committed, the criminal justice systems of capitalist societies are almost always prepared to attribute guilt to a single individual.

As to each point, Africans refuse to follow the script because of cultural attributes that are centuries older than their sojourn in western capitalist countries. Even upwardly mobile Africans do not generally look out for self and self alone. When they hear that their nephew Ray-Ray has been arrested yet again, they dole out bail money without hesitation. When Grand Aunt Mae Belle can't pay the landlord this month, they write a check. In fact, it has been suggested that it is this sense of family and community obligation that accounts to a significant degree for the continuing gap in wealth between similarly situated white and black professionals.

Likewise, accomplishments are rarely regarded as the sole result of individual effort in African communities. Brothers in the barbershop who marvel over the piece in Jet Magazine about a newly-appointed black CEO of a Fortune 500 company will congratulate each other for the progress that "we" are making (even though they have never met the executive they are talking about). The African diasporan community regards itself as a collective that shares both benefits and burdens. This way of thinking is straight out of traditional Africa, and when it traveled west with enslaved Africans, it refused to let go. In traditional Africa, if one member of a village causes harm to another village, the offender's entire village assumes responsibility for the misdeed.

African notions of collective responsibility have also been the source of great frustration and confusion for Africans in the diaspora. Africans have spent countless hours contemplating slavery, its impact and implications. With their collective African mind, they have collectively reached the African conclusion that inasmuch as slavery victimized a distinct group of people, and a distinct group of people benefitted from it (and in many ways continue to benefit from it) then there should be a collective remedy for slavery's harm that should be provided collectively by those who were beneficiaries of slavery as an institution.

However, "reparations" is a dirty word in much of the white world because to a far larger extent, white people have fully embraced and internalized the capitalist principle of individualism. Collective guilt as a concept offends them at the most basic level. The mere mention of reparations triggers an almost reflexive response that contemporary white individuals never owned slaves and cannot be held accountable for the sins of their ancestors. If pressed, they will even insist that reparations advocates identify individual Africans in Africa who cooperated with slave traders and demand reparations from them as well.

Our analysis here is not about the merits of reparations, and we will not dwell on the many ways in which even contemporary white individuals continue to unfairly benefit from social dynamics, economic advantage and political structures that originated in slavery. Suffice it to say that this tension reflects a deeper conflict between a fundamental approach to human relationships urged by Jesus and an opposing, self-centered approach that has been thoroughly transformed by capitalism from vice into virtue. The stubborn insistence by the collective African community on maintaining community and resisting pressures to adopt individualism is a blow that Satan feels in significant ways.

In a number of other ways the African community has declined to accept capitalist views and principles. Greed (which capitalists call by other names) is an important capitalist value. Over the years, Africans have been proportionately more generous than other groups when it comes to giving their money to charities and their time to community service. There is an emphasis within the African community on sharing. This is as true for those with almost nothing in the way of material possessions as it is for African celebrities who often, and without fanfare, support many people from their old neighborhoods and elsewhere.

Finally, and perhaps because Africans have been the victims of ruthless behavior for so long, as a group they have been unwilling to elevate themselves at the expense of others. Capitalism urges that profits be pursued without sentimentality.

If this can only be accomplished by destroying others, then so be it. However Africans have rarely - if ever - developed a calculated plan for their own empowerment that would leave another ethnic or racial group by the wayside.

As a matter of fact, in those cases when Africans have been pitted against Koreans, Mexicans, Arabs and other ethnic groups (depending upon the region of the country) they have been unwitting pawns, along with the groups they have opposed, in schemes hatched by unseen capitalists to dis-empower both communities of color that took bait that led them into artificially created conflicts. For example, if Africans born in America have been the bulk of the labor force in a particular industry for several generations, and they have come to expect wages that keep pace with inflation, smart capitalists will begin to hire other ethnic immigrants for lower wages. Rather than blame the capitalists, Africans will blame the other ethnic group for "taking jobs." Meanwhile the unseen capitalists take special pleasure in watching powerless communities blame each other for capitalist mischief.

It is ironic that sometimes, materialist philosophers who ignore or deny the spiritual realm are the most adept at making a spiritual analysis without recognizing that they have done so.

For example, Karl Marx posited as a scientific fact that within a capitalist society, the injustices and contradictions of the system would eventually lead the workers to rise up and destroy capitalism. What Marx knew and included as a factor in his analysis is that within most human beings there is an instinctive love of justice. This love of justice causes people to reject injustice in every respect - especially when it comes to economics. Although Marx and other materialists may have been unwilling to identify it as such, the love of justice that resides within most human beings is God. Because Satan is unwilling to forego an attack on God wherever he may be found, Satan enters the human consciousness and effectively brings the spiritual war into each individual. For each human being the question of greatest importance is, in this internal spiritual war, who will prevail - God or Satan? For the most part, God holds sway among Africans.

In suggesting that God's influence is dominant among Africans, it is not suggested that they are a perfect people. In matters of personal morality, it is easy to see the failings of Africans. Drive-by shootings, obscene rap lyrics and videos, bourgeois elitism, and much more most certainly do not meet with God's approval. However, on a deeper more fundamental level, Africans as a group have limits that constrain their behavior, and it can be suggested with some degree of comfort that these limits are God-inspired.

To be more concrete, for all of the crimes committed by Africans, and that are reported in the media, most are pedestrian (without of course minimizing the profound negative impact of any crime). Crimes that involve mass killings, satanic rituals, depraved sex acts, and the murder of children, are widely regarded as taboo in the African community. If such crimes are committed with any regularity by Africans, they are certainly rarely reported. It is more likely that they rarely occur.

In fact, it is a matter of no small concern among African elders that at some point, the African sojourn in the diaspora will finally take its toll, and taboos will fall, and Africans will descend into a level of immorality that has been heretofore unseen. How many times have we heard an elder comment: "It's too bad that happened, but I'm glad it wasn't none of our children that did it. If the news man had reported that it was black boys who went in that school and killed all those children, then I would have said that we are just lost as a people."

Discussion of comparative moral standards is presented in a discussion about capitalism primarily because it relates to the potential of Africans to lead the rest of the society away from that economic system. This is particularly important because of inroads that Satan has made into the white religious community with respect to economics. Within the white religious right it is sometimes difficult to discern whether there is greater reverence for God or the capitalist system. Leaders of the white religious right are sometimes indistinguishable from right wing politicians except for the occasional references they make to the Bible.

In many ways, the Church is the final frontier for Satan. If he succeeds in fully and finally establishing that capitalism is morally superior to what is presented as the only alternative – "Godless Communism," then there will be very little resistance. The African religious community has long held the line against endorsement of capitalist principles. Africans have rejected notions of greed and selfishness, and through their churches they have bankrolled and administered numerous charitable operations. African Christian ministers were profiles in courage and principle as they led civil rights movement demonstrations.

Yet, in the 21st century, even the African Christian community is at risk. A number of African "prosperity preachers" have huge congregations, and tremendous time is spent on the subject of acquiring wealth. It is this and other developments that are a signal to the spiritual warriors of the African community that there has been a breach in our barricade, and they will have to become increasingly vigilant.

Chapter Ten

Fissures in African Spiritual Armor

Spiritual armor worn by Africans has shielded them from the most relentless evil attacks, but we are compelled to take note of what may be fissures in the armor and to sound an alarm before there is a total rupture.

In the preceding chapter we considered the perceived, if not actual, moral limits of African behavior. As noted, crime and social pathologies that afflict elements of the black community (e.g., drug addiction, prostitution, gang violence, theft, etc.) rarely, if ever, produce serial killers or sick individuals like Jeffrey Dahmer who not only murdered and tortured a series of victims, but also cannibalized them. These types of individuals have been truly and thoroughly taken over by satanic forces, and such evil influences have rarely penetrated African spiritual defenses.

This is intuitively understood in African communities, and it is not uncommon to hear pronouncements such as: "Lawd, chile, when I heard them say on the news that they were trying to find a serial killer, they could ask me and I could tell 'em, well he ain't black." This common belief was shaken a bit when the world learned that the "D.C. Sniper" was John Muhammad, a black man. But the relative certainty that Africans don't commit such crimes remains prevalent.

The measure of whether Satan has penetrated African spiritual defenses is not found in the commission of particular evil acts. The existence of a D.C. Sniper, or a black woman who sells her five year old daughter into prostitution are reasons to be highly alarmed, but they indicate a spiritual breakdown for individuals and not an entire community. To gauge the moral integrity of the collective community it is necessary to examine the culture and its manifestations.

When white communities produce evil individuals, examination of their lifestyles, associates or the literature they read will often explain how and why they chose to launch a killing spree or engage in other unconscionable acts. In one case the individual may have been part of a satanic cult. In another case they may have been engaged in witchcraft. Many individuals drift into the occult on a whim and as a lark. Among segments of white youth in particular this type of activity has a special appeal, perhaps because it appeals to adolescent rebellious impulses. For example, many of them strive to acquire or maintain a very pale complexion that stands in dramatic contrast to all black "Goth" clothing that they wear daily. Others are fascinated by vampire culture.

Kids may take up these lifestyles for kicks or to get attention, but the occult is nothing to play with. What begins as innocent fun becomes an opening for Satan's mischief. Individuals who isolate themselves from more Godly people and ideas become easy prey. They can be sucked deeper and deeper into a twisted view of God and humanity. Violent and perverted acts begin to appear not only rational, but essential.

The Columbine high school killing spree was committed by two boys who, according to reports, had become obsessed with very dark video games. There was speculation that their chronic exposure to violent video images desensitized them to the value of human life, and made random murder an easy reaction to whatever delusions of injustice they were convinced that they had suffered.

Occult-influenced video games are not the only medium by which Satan has gained access to juvenile minds. There is also heavy-metal music and its videos, as well as certain movies and other aspects of popular culture that present themselves as harmless fun, but which can actually stimulate very evil, if not dangerous behavior.

One government reaction to mass violence was the Gun Free Schools Act, which is popularly known as the "Zero Tolerance" law. It essentially requires the immediate expulsion of any student who brings a firearm on to school property. The irony is that the type of school violence that inspired the law was caused primarily by white youth. Yet, the expulsion statistics tend to disproportionately affect African students.

As noted, Africans have engaged in numerous violent acts. But the collective concern must be with the causes of those acts. The collective moral and spiritual health of the African community remains intact as long as the evil acts of African individuals are isolated and the result of: insanity, addiction-induced desperation, youthful impulse, peer pressure and other human failings brought on by natural human frailty. With few exceptions, the most notorious Africans who have committed heinous crimes have done so because of such causes.

Our concern must become elevated if Africans' crimes become manifestations of evil doctrines or creeds of cults or a particular belief system. To date, philosophies that are explicitly satanic have not gained significant traction in African communities. However, there are fissures into which the forces of evil can insinuate themselves unless those with moral strength act quickly to reinforce the spiritual structure.

Young African children - particularly boys- are not insulated from video games that have dark, violent themes. These games, many of which are portable, apparently have addictive qualities. Children become locked in a seemingly hypnotic trance while manipulating hand-held electronic game devices. Their parents look on in frustration as they recall their own childhoods when they spent every free waking moment engaged in active outdoor play. Hour after hour, children participate in wild, gory, virtual combat. Heads are blown off. Limbs are severed. Torsos explode into countless bloody shreds. It begins to have an effect.

Likewise, graphic music and music videos that glorify gang violence can desensitize viewers to the actual consequences of firearms. As just one example, a thoughtful, wrongly imprisoned political activist once asked a younger black prisoner to describe his emotions after listening to particularly violent gangster rap. The young prisoner responded: "That song makes me want to go out and kill a nigga."

Young Africans are not the only ones at risk. Some older Africans, out of resentment or other emotion-driven motives, deliberately turn their backs on traditional churches and embark on a spiritual search. They may find themselves at "new age" retreats or among the ranks of other novel spiritual formations. While some of these associations may be based on the most positive values, others may be only a half step away from demonic influences. Most dangerous are cults that achieve undue psychological influence over members.

At present, individuals and societies that are explicitly devoted to evil doctrines or that engage in occult rituals are still regarded by the overwhelming majority of Africans as "weird" spiritual enemies. However, this can change as young African children increasingly identify with some white peers who are being raised in communities where dark ideas are considered hip and trendy. It is this predicament that illustrates particularly well the vital importance of cultural identity and the dangers of presuming that assimilation into the culture of the majority is in some way an effective method of addressing "the race problem."

In the end, African communities will know that they are in real trouble if a generation begins to celebrate the occult. The community's best defense is constant reinforcement of a shared understanding of the battle lines that exist between the forces of good and evil. Likewise there is a supremely important place in

126

this struggle for aggressive unapologetic parental censoring of the media and popular culture consumed by children.

Chapter Eleven

Conclusion:
The Certainty of Victory

God demonstrates his love for us in more ways than a human being is able to count. Nevertheless, one of the greatest gifts that he has given us is the Bible - a document that explains not only the history of God's great conflict with evil forces but also a detailed account of how it all ends. The book of Revelation frightens many, but it is actually God's way of saying that everything is going to be alright. It is a remarkable and wonderful message that allows us to confront a terrifying world with complete confidence that Satan will ultimately be defeated.

Many people of faith are confused by Revelation. They analyze it with human understanding and presume that because it concerns the future, it is not an account of observed events, but rather God's "plan" for how events will one day unfold. They then become quite disturbed because they cannot understand why God would *plan* the cataclysmic, catastrophic events in Revelation.

However, we must never lose sight of the fact that our human perceptions and experiences are not always identical to God's. We experience "time" as an unalterable sequence of moments - one following the other always, into eternity. God on the other hand moves easily back and forth through time. When he tells us what will happen in the future, he does not manipulate developments to fit his script. Rather, he has simply visited the future, observed what will happen and then reported back to us.

The word "report" is key because God has only observed what we, as beings with free will, have chosen to do. So while we can take comfort in the knowledge that good will triumph over evil, we can be no less diligent in our personal efforts to play our role in this scenario. Victory will happen only because we have fought as hard as we can fight to fulfill our mission.

Knowing that we shall prevail should also embolden us as we move through life. Not only can we be confident of victory, but we can also be confident that God desperately wants to win this war and he is standing by always to assist and defend us as we work on his behalf. For Africans, the proof is in their history notwithstanding the repeated assertion that they bear a "curse." If there is a curse, it is not one imposed by God. Satan on the other hand took special note of the close collective relationship that Africans have with God, and he has made it his business to create every conceivable horror for this spiritual people. But notwithstanding Satan's most vicious attacks, God has always been there to prop Africans up when they have been knocked down, and to give them the fortitude to strike back.

It was God who made it possible for beaten slaves to stand up and survive. It was God who allowed runaway slaves to escape. It was God who miraculously propelled Africans into political leadership during Reconstruction, and who prevented their extermination when Satan inspired a white backlash that manifested itself in the creation of the Ku Klux Klan and an epidemic of lynching. It was God who gave Civil Rights protesters the unbelievable courage to face armed police, fire hoses, attack dogs, and murderous mobs. It was God who, against all odds, allowed an African to rise to the position of head of state, and to live with his beautiful family in a big white house that was built by slaves.

By no means has Satan given up on his quest to destroy a God-fearing, God-loving people. The road ahead for Africans in the diaspora is filled with great challenges, heartbreak and hardship. But because Africans know that God will be with them as he has been through the generations, most who walk this road

130

know that victory is certain, and though they have traveled far they are always ready to declare: "I ain't got tired yet."[25]

Appendix of Essays
On African Dignity, Character and Self-Respect

African Women, White Men, Sex and Don Imus

This essay was originally published in the midst of a public scandal triggered by radio personality Don Imus' reference to the predominantly black Rutgers University women's basketball team as "nappy-headed ho's." Some pundits suggested that the misogynist lyrics of Hip-Hop music gave Imus license to use such language.

It is likely that on countless street corners throughout America, young Africans continue to ponder with great bewilderment how a crusty old racist with a radio show caused the national spotlight to focus on them and what they believe to be their music. Imus's vile pronouncement that the women of Rutgers' basketball team are "nappy-headed hos" triggered expected condemnation from "Black Leadership." But like a tornado that first wreaks havoc on a trailer park and then skips gingerly across several miles of grasslands before causing more destruction in a distant location, the leaders' criticism moved swiftly from Imus, landed at Hip-Hop's door, and lingered there.

The misogyny and self-loathing racial references of Hip-Hop are indefensible, and "Black Leadership's" instincts were on target. However, Africans in America find themselves in a moment when the struggles for liberation, human rights and justice demand that every blow that a "leader" strikes for the people enjoy the benefit of informed analysis rooted in an accurate understanding of history. It is no longer enough to simply point fingers at rap artists whose lyrics reference "hos" and "bitches" and somehow imply that Imus was inspired by African youth. Very basic questions must first be asked about whether Hip-Hop recordings released by mega entertainment corporations represent the honest expression of African youth culture, or whether they are instead products of white middle-aged executive male fantasies that have been tailored to appeal to the white, suburban teenaged demographic that accounts for more than three-quarters of all Hip-Hop music sales. Questions must then be asked about what drives the handful of young African "artists" who engage in Hip-Hop minstrelsy.

Even the most cursory research reveals that the Imus affair is but a 21st Century manifestation of a white American pathology that has very deep historical roots. From the earliest days of their nightmarish, but nevertheless glorious sojourn in the western hemisphere, African women have been pegged as "hos" without any regard for their actual conduct. In a well-researched little book titled Ar'n't I a Woman?, historian Deborah Gray White described not only the experiences of African women on slave plantations, but also the attitudes held by white society. She wrote: "One of the most prevalent images of black women in antebellum America was of a person governed almost entirely by her libido, a Jezebel character."

White explained how proponents of the Jezebel idea used African dance styles, African women's sparse tropical clothing, and instances of polygamy as evidence of lust and lewdness. Victorian-era white women who dressed in layers of satin and lace looked with disdain on African women who tied their skirts around their upper thighs as they labored in water-filled rice fields. White men who took to routinely referring to African women as "wenches" convinced themselves that every African female they encountered looked upon them with lust. White quoted one white visitor to the antebellum south as stating: "...in almost every house there are negresses, slaves, who count it an honor to bring a mulatto into the world." This notion of black female sexuality became the foundation for an unspeakable history of mass rape. Countless enslaved African families endured the horror of having slave masters break into their homes and sexually assault a mother, or even pubescent and pre-pubescent daughters - sometimes as the family watched in helpless terror.

There is much about the slave era that Africans themselves internalized. The word "nigger" became not only a derogatory word that accompanied acts of racial terrorism, but also a word long used by Africans themselves as a term of endearment. It is but one of numerous manifestations of self-hatred and a widely-shared inferiority complex. It is no wonder then that African men and many African women also internalized racist notions of black female sexuality.

While some might suggest that Hip-Hop misogyny is entirely home-grown, history indicates that the denigration of women is at odds with much of the culture of traditional Africa. For example, men not only recognized the genius of the Angolan queen, Nzinga, but also followed her into battle repeatedly in an ongoing war against the Portuguese. Likewise, the Ashanti Queen Mother Yaa Asantewa enjoyed universal respect, as did many other African queens. Among even the common folk, matrilineal succession was a distinct feature of certain traditional ethnic communities. As Africa's cultures were impacted by Arab and European influences, attitudes toward women changed. U.S. male chauvinism has certainly affected the attitudes of African males in America, including those who are willing to use the worst names for their sisters in recordings that they make for large corporations.

While it is important to remain vigilant in the quest to purge Hip-Hop of its misogynist language, and racial self-hatred, it is perhaps most helpful to be armed with an analysis of its origins. The young brothers on the block who are puzzled about why they are being blamed for Don Imus's racism deserve a complete, informed explanation and not just finger-wagging condemnation.

House Slaves, Field Slaves and
the Obama Predicament

This essay was originally published in the midst of the 2008 Presidential Campaign.

In his book, *Africa and Africans in the Making of the Atlantic World, 1400 - 1800*, author John Thornton confirms the long-held anecdotal presumption that enslaved Africans who worked in the plantation "big house" had a better quality of life than those who worked in the fields.

Thornton states:

> The contrast between the life of a domestic servant, residing in the owner's house, perhaps well dressed and not necessarily overworked, and that of the plantation slaves and field hands is well illustrated by the case of two Brazilian domestics, Ines and Juliana. These two pampered slaves, raised among the Europeans and sharing in their lives, testified against their master, Paulo Affonso, to the Inquisition of Bahia in 1613-14, and in reprisal, their master ordered them transferred as field hands to his sugar estate at Itapianga. There, a short time later they were both dead, victims of 'many whippings and bad life and labor.

It is likely that as a consequence of these and comparable incidents, many enslaved Africans who toiled and suffered in the fields recognized their limited life options, and set their sights on a place on the master's domestic staff. If the fate of Sisters Ines and Juliana is any indication, disloyalty, insolence and recalcitrance were not qualities that were tolerated in a house slave, and a slave could win a coveted position in the big house only if he or she could assure the master that there would be no efforts to slip poison into the slave owner's food, or kill him as he slept.

However, masters had no guarantee of docility. In his book *Runaway Slaves*, distinguished historian John Hope Franklin observed:

> Even slaves who were thought to be mild mannered and obedient sometimes reached a breaking point. Having never reacted violently, the house servant of a Louisiana woman 'returned the blow' as she was being physically chastised by her owner, threw her mistress to the ground, and 'beat her unmercifully, on the head and face.' The white woman's face swelled up and turned black. 'I could not have known her, by seeing her,' a visitor at the plantation said a few weeks later, 'poor little woman is confined to bed yet' and remains 'dangerously ill'.

Thus, a house slave - or an African who aspired to become a house slave - was faced with the choice of either pleasing the master at all costs in order to preserve a relatively privileged position; or, resolve that even if there were benefits to living under the master's roof, they were not worth losing the little bit of dignity and self-respect that even a slave might have if he or she was willing to fight for them.

Africans may have ultimately moved off of the plantation, but many continue to seek their place in the big house. Modern big houses may be executive positions in major corporations – or even entry level jobs. A big house might be tenure on a university faculty, or a partnership in a major law firm. The shared characteristic of all of these "big houses" is that in some way, shape or form, the aspirant must gain favor with gatekeepers.

To accomplish this, Africans must frequently suppress or conceal much about themselves that connects them to their culture. Speech patterns and slang used at home give way to "corporation speak." Otherwise natural hair is relaxed. Jokes told in the board room that aren't funny to most Africans are laughed at anyway. A brother who might normally prefer to spend Saturday afternoon shooting hoops will grudgingly find himself on the golf course with his white co-workers.

Barack Obama's efforts to enter the biggest of big houses in American politics has allowed us to see in the clearest way possible that the price of access is doing whatever it takes to make white people like you. Thus, Obama has found himself in the pathetic position, of essentially trudging through rural America with hat in hand, trying to convince white people – many of them bigots – that he is "safe," and not at all like those "other blacks." Reverend Jeremiah Wright's rhetoric has been blamed for having a destructive impact on the Obama campaign. But the truth is, if the pastor had never spoken a word, in the minds of white America, Wright's mere presence, would still have proclaimed: "Obama is just like all of those other Negroes!"

What's more, it has been interesting to observe how so many Africans who have come to identify strongly with the Obama campaign react when Reverend Wright or anyone else actually says things that threaten to shatter the illusion of the "black man who isn't black." In one form or another, we have heard a loud chorus of: "Hush now! Don't let them white folks hear you!"

Has it really come to this? Have our people forgotten that Malcolm X, the Panthers, John Carlos, Tommie Smith, Kwame

Ture and countless others stood up so that we would never again have to kneel meekly before "The Man"? What happened? Have our people on a mass level adopted a house slave mentality? Not likely. After all, the Detroit Branch of the NAACP and 11,000 Africans who attended its Freedom Fund Dinner, displayed the spirit of the field slave when they welcomed Reverend Wright into their presence as an act of defiance. Not only that, there are no doubt millions of other Africans who agree with every word Reverend Wright has uttered.

No, the irony is that in many cases, the near fanatic support for Obama (notwithstanding the candidate's obsession with calming white fears) is in many cases fueled by field slave impulses. In general, those impulses drive the field slave to take that which is forbidden, to walk through doors that have been locked, and to (whenever possible) rub success in the face of the oppressor. As the field slaves watch Obama march steadily toward a position that a black man is not supposed to have until the passage of at least another generation, they can't help but get caught up.

Only time will tell whether the unrelenting beating that Obama has taken in recent weeks for no reason other than he happens to be African will be the cold slap in the face that reminds the slaves out in the field that merely becoming a resident of the big house does not transform the new occupant into the master. Although many see value – even if only sentimental or symbolic– in electing a black president, it should become increasingly apparent that if the quest for a position in the big house compels a slave to abandon his pastor, ignore his community, commit to a corporate and Zionist agenda, and pander to bigots, then it is likely that once he moves in, he will have to stay with that program if he wants to keep his job.

On the plantation, it is likely that many of the field slaves who managed to talk their way into the big house entered fully conscious of the likelihood that the humiliation they would suffer there would reach intolerable limits. Those contemporary field slaves who live vicariously through would-be President Obama, will be well advised to, like their ancestors, continue their journey toward 1600 Pennsylvania Avenue with open eyes, and a frank realization that the presidency is not a political panacea – and possibly not even a palliative pill for the ills of America's African population. If we are to achieve genuine liberation, all political options, including revolution must not only remain open, but be pursued as though the world had never heard of Barack Obama.

Author's Note: When it was first published, this essay was likely regarded by some as a criticism, or even an attack on Barack Obama. It was not intended so much as an attack as it was a frank assessment of his predicament. The truth is, I have always liked the image projected by then-candidate, and now-President Obama and his beautiful family. The "smarter-than-everybody-in-the-room-cool-as-a-cucumber" profile that he strikes has done wonders for black self-esteem, and has inspired high aspirations among our youth. But at the same time we can't kid ourselves about his circumstances. The United States government is designed to preserve an empire, and all who lead it must sign on committed to that mission. So in the end, President Obama is in the same boat as all of the rest of us who sell our labor to institutions that may have missions inconsistent with our own. The only question always is whether we have not only sold our labor, but also sold our souls.

Kip's Folly

Army General William E. "Kip" Ward stands tall as imperialism's shining black prince. He has been anointed to head Africom, a rapidly unfolding plan to establish an expanded western military presence in Africa for the purpose of securing domination of the continent's oil and other natural resources. (Okay, okay - so they claim Africom is designed to quell internal strife and fight terrorism. But none of us believe that.)

Although Africom has triggered a wave of grumbling across the breadth of the African continent and into many corners of the African Diaspora, it's a pretty good bet that from the oil company executive suites, to the oval office, to the Pentagon, and on down to the fellas who hang out in the officer's club at the local Army base, General Ward is the man of the hour. Even his nickname has been made to order. Can't you hear the comments? "That Kip is a credit to his country, the armed forces and his race." "Why can't they all be more like Kip?"

With degrees from Morgan State University and Pennsylvania State University followed by 36 years of military service in Korea, Egypt, Somalia, Bosnia, Israel, Germany, Alaska and Hawaii, how can you beat this guy? He certainly must have been the kind of person retired generals had in mind when, during the last big affirmative action case to come before the Supreme Court the generals said:"... the military cannot achieve an officer corps that is both highly qualified and racially diverse" without race-conscious remedies. And if the military can't do that, whose black faces can be used to give credibility to U.S. military operations in Africa?

It is certainly possible that General Ward is a dedicated career military man who, with great sincerity, welcomes the opportunity to cap his long career with service to the continent of his ancestral origins. If so, that is precisely the problem. He and so many Africans born in America who have distinguished themselves professionally within corporate and government structures either naively miss, or deliberately ignore, their drift into roles that require them to work against the interests of their people.

In the case of Africom, this project is not divorced from a long history of efforts by Africa's people to wrest control of unquantifiable natural wealth, first from western governments that colonized the continent and more recently from multi-national corporations that exploit Africa with the assistance of black neo-colonial heads of African states. It has been necessary for many of these people's struggles to be carried out with arms in places like Angola, Guinea Bissau, Congo, Mozambique and

146

Zimbabwe. Given the determination of exploiters to maintain their iron grip on valuable natural resources, even while Africa's people suffer and starve, it is certainly likely that armed struggle by genuine revolutionaries will occur again in other parts of the continent. When that happens, we can safely bet that the Pentagon will label the African freedom fighters as terrorists and order good ole Kip to "suppress the restless natives."

General Ward is not alone in his willingness to play the role of imperialist lackey. Barack Obama enthusiastically embraces the Africom concept. He uttered the following nonsense: "There will be situations that require the United States to work with its partners in Africa to fight terrorism with lethal force. Having a unified command operating in Africa will facilitate this action." If Ward and Obama were to rationalize their compromises with the tired excuse that Africom can't be stopped and "at least it will be under the control of a brother," we would be compelled to respond that our people's history shows that it doesn't have to be that way.

At the dawn of the 20th Century, when Buffalo Soldiers were directed by racist white commanders to suppress a rebellion by brown-skinned Filipinos, conscience prevented a number of these Africans from following those orders. During the Vietnam War, some of the brothers in the U.S. military did the same thing.

In fact, Muhammad Ali, while at the peak of his career, was moved by conscience to bravely refuse to fight in Vietnam. He lost almost everything as a consequence. We must remember the 43 brothers in the Marines stationed at Fort Hood, Texas who were prosecuted for refusing to attack anti-war protesters at the 1968 Democratic National Convention.

This tradition of refusing to participate in unconscionable U.S. military missions is alive even today. Consider that until the year 2000, U.S.-born Africans accounted for nearly 25 percent of Army personnel. By 2004, less than 16 percent of Army recruits were Africans. That percentage continues to decline. An Army study concluded that the attitudes of black youth were significantly shaped by their community, and the widespread opposition to the Iraq War in that community led to a rejection of military service. According to a Gallup Poll, 78 percent of whites supported the Iraq war, and 72 percent of blacks opposed it in 2003.

Is it fair to demand that Ward commit career suicide by opposing Africom, or at least refusing to lead it? The short answer is yes. Since our arrival on U.S. shores, Africans have never had the convenient option of declining heroism. Unlike the majority demographic in this country whose individual decisions often have implications only for the individuals who make them, whenever we Africans take the easy road paved by an oppressive system, large numbers of our people are injured or killed as a consequence. Contemplate for only a moment the incredible number of lives of oppressed people and people of color that have been ruined or lost because of the opportunistic, self-centered careers of Clarence Thomas, Condoleezza Rice, and other lesser-known individuals of that ilk. General Ward stands poised to preside over an operation that possibly poses the most lethal threat to Africa and African people in the modern era. If on the question of whether to go forward as Africom's commander, Ward is to be guided by morality and his people's history, he has but one clear choice.

About the Author

For the entirety of his 26 years of practicing law, Mark P. Fancher's client list has been dominated by workers, the poor and individuals whose human or civil rights have been violated in one way or another. The courts have been a forum where he has been able to plead his clients' individual causes. But because he is also dedicated to fighting for African liberation he has routinely moved beyond the courthouse and into the streets to argue to all who will listen that all Africans and people of African descent throughout the world will be free when foreign corporations are expelled from the African continent and a single, socialist African government is established. Fancher has worked with various organizations that share this objective, and he has authored many essays, pamphlets and books about Pan-Africanism. This book represents his first public discussion of the spiritual faith that sustains him and that has sustained many of his Christian, Pan-Africanist predecessors for generations. Fancher is a member of Bethel African Methodist Episcopal Church in Ann Arbor, Michigan.

NOTES FROM PRIMARY TEXT

1. *The Politics of Jesus*, Obery Hendricks, Doubleday (2006) p. 9.

2. See *Runaway Slaves*, John Hope Franklin, Oxford University Press (1999).

3. *African Religions and Philosophy*, John S. Mbiti, Heinemann Educational Publishers (1969) p. 29.

4. *The Lost Cities of Africa*, Basil Davidson, Little Brown (1959) pp. 90-93.

5. *Black Athena: The Afroasiatic Roots of Classical Civilization*, Martin Bernal, Rutgers University Press (1987).

6. *Blacks In Science - Ancient and Modern*, edited by Ivan Van Sertima, Transaction Books (1983).

7. *Black Athena* (supra) p. 201 - 202.

8. *Id.* at 241.

9. *Id.* (quoting 19th Century naturalist Baron Cuvier).

10. Id. (quoting 19th Century scholar Comte de Gobineau).

11. *Slavery by Another Name*, Douglas A. Blackmon, Doubleday (2008) p.45.

12. *The Days When the Animals Talked*, William John Faulkner (1977) p. 54 (as quoted in *Slave Culture*, Sterling Stuckey, Oxford University Press (1987) p. 33.

13. *Denmark Vesey: The Buried Story of America's Largest Slave Rebellion and the Man Who Led It*, David Robertson, Vintage Books (1999) p. 47.

14. *Id.* at 48.

15. *Ready for Revolution*, Kwame Ture with Ekwueme Michael Thelwell, Scribner (2003) p. 771.

16. *Id.*

17. *An Unbroken Agony*, Randall Robinson, Basic Civitas Books (2007), 92.

18. *Id.* at 77-78.

19. *Maurice Bishop Speaks*, Pathfinder Press (1983) p. 64.

20. *Jamaica Under Manley*, by Michael Kaufman, Lawrence Hill and Company (1985) p. 71.

21. *African Science in School Curriculum*, by Brian Murfin (copy of excerpt on file with the author).

22. See: *Blacks In Science - Ancient and Modern*, edited by Ivan Van Sertima, Transaction Books (1983).

23. *African Science in School Curriculum*, by Brian Murfin (copy of excerpt on file with the author.)

24. *The Souls of Black Folk*, by W.E.B. DuBois, Fawcett Publications (1961) (originally published in 1903) pp. 142-143.

25. The author offers special thanks to his parents Dr. Charles B. Fancher, Sr. and Dr. Evelyn P. Fancher who generously offered their informed and very helpful critiques of an unpublished draft of this book. He also sends a shout-out and a big thank you to his lovely, loving wife Lorray S.C. Brown, and his brilliant, wonderful little son, Toussaint.